DO YOU WANT TO BE A

LEADER OR A MANAGER?

If You Can Do One, You Can Do Both....

By

Jack Finnell

Dedicated to Gail Brown Finnell, Annie Finnell Grant and John Edward Finnell, the three people I admire most.

"I am a young engineer, just starting her career. Jack has years of leadership experience, beginning when he was thrown into the deep end as a young Navy officer. I can actually put his advice and tips into practice with real world examples. His stories have helped me to internalize the lessons he shares and better understand how I could actually implement these tools in my own career. He has armed me with tools you can't get from an MBA."

EMMA BENJAMINSON, MIT Graduate, Mechanical Engineer I at Glaucos Corporation

"Jack Finnell's military background, success at a Fortune 500 company and years building his own business from the ground up culminating in a successful sale to a billion-dollar suitor and then heading back to carrying a bag at a multi-billion-dollar consulting firm has given him a unique perspective on management from both sides of the desk. Jack's lessons are comprehensive and appropriate for those just starting in their first leadership role to seasoned CEOs – anyone leading a team will benefit."

TOM FEDRO, CEO Paragon Software Group

"Jack helps Leaders become more effective Managers. Great personal stories here. I highly recommend."

MONICA LEE COPELAND, Chief Development & Marketing Officer Cerritos College Foundation

"With Jack Finnell's knowledge, experience, intensity and passion, it's easy to understand why people stop to pay attention to what he has to say. As a result of executing on his insight, I've been able to dramatically increase revenue and improve the effectiveness of my team."

MICHAEL JAKMAKJIAN, Technology Sales Executive

"Jack makes it clear that what Leadership & Management Excellence is all about are these 2 things: Spike the Numbers and Curtail Key Employee Turnover. As a CEO, do I find his lessons helpful? Yup."

JOEL HACKETT, President QDOXS

CONTENTS

Introduction 9

ARE LEADERS and MANAGERS DIFFERENT? 11

How Effective Managers Become Better Leaders 17

How Do Natural Leaders Become Better Managers? 52

Corporate Politics – Of *Course*, It Exists................................102

About the Author..115

Acknowledgements 116

INTRODUCTION

This book is based on my leadership and management experience in the U.S. Navy, a couple of multi-billion-dollar tech companies and two successful tech start-ups that my business partner and I sold to publicly traded corporations.

Right after college and the Navy, I had a highly productive thirteen-year career at a Fortune 100 company where I was the Number One Branch Manager in the U.S. in two different locations: Alaska and L.A. South. I knew I wasn't the smartest manager around nor the most inspirational leader. Still, I couldn't deny that something was going on to pull that off twice in wildly different markets with 110 FTEs in Alaska and 330 in L.A. South. I figured it out: all along I have been identifying, cataloguing and mastering certain successful activities, behaviors and techniques and then passing these on to my direct reports through one-on-one developmental sessions, formal and informal. These activities and techniques all have two goals: Spike the Numbers and Curtail Employee Turnover. About 30 per cent of what I have mastered and passed on popped out of my own head. The other 70 per cent or so came from other men and women I've worked with over the years. However, I have personally field-tested all of the lessons I'm passing on in this book. I know they work, and I hope the real-world stories I offer here will make these lessons credible and indelible for you.

CHAPTER 1

ARE LEADERS AND MANAGERS

DIFFERENT?

We think so, don't we? Leaders inspire, and managers execute, right? Some people seem to be good at one role and not so hot at the other. Well, let me assure you right now – you absolutely **can** perform both roles effectively. You don't even have to change who you are. You **will** need to concentrate on certain activities and techniques that anyone who wants to can master. Stand by...

Of course, top performers don't always want to manage or lead. Would you rather be the star center fielder or the team manager? Maybe that one's too obvious, so I asked my daughter, Annie, "Would you rather be the star kindergarten teacher or the school principal?" She really likes her principal but told me she loved being the one who turns on the lights for these 5-year olds, teaching them math and reading and writing. It's too fun and stimulating for her, and she doesn't want to give it up. Maybe someday, but not now. And she can see that her friend the principal has to put up with a considerable amount of grief from parents that she'd rather bypass.

Of course, some top performers are innately great and can't pass it on to others...or just don't care to. The motivation to be a manager or a leader does matter, so be honest about it.

Remember, managers and leaders are not superior to strong performers. In fact, without strong performers, managers and leaders cannot succeed at all, can they? There are plenty of acceptable motivations to lead and manage: enjoy challenges, want to create positive change on a broader scale, like to trigger the best in people just for the satisfaction of it. There's only one bad motivation: "I'm better than everyone else, so I should be the boss." Please, spare us, because you'll just make yourself miserable, too.

Now, what do managers and leaders do – managers first.

The classic definition of management, and it still works, is this: **Managers accomplish work through other people.** This book, as you can tell, is not a formal economic or business treatise. Still, it's good to remember the four basic management functions, because they're useful and real-world:

1. Plan and Organize
2. Communicate
3. Implement
4. Control and Track

Managers PLAN the business by defining the strategies, tactics and out-comes, and they ORGANIZE the financial and human resources to achieve them. Then they COMMUNICATE the plan to their bosses, to their associates in adjacent departments, to their direct reports and to the marketplace. Next, they go out and IMPLEMENT those plans internally and externally. Finally, they CONTROL and TRACK the activities and results to ensure the plans are producing the desired performance, as in, "If you can't measure it, you can't manage it."

Yup, managers execute tasks and objectives. To accomplish work that requires people, someone has to pull them together and define the tasks. For efficiency and effectiveness, managers set the business objectives, hire people with the requisite skills, train them and give them feedback on their progress. Excellent managers know the work itself, how to teach it and how to handle problems that interfere with it.

Now, this is important: do you know what all employees - including you and me - care about most when sizing up their managers? Just one thing: **"Does he help me or hurt me?"**

My good friend and former business partner, Tom, taught me that one years ago, and I never forgot it. It's one hundred per cent true, isn't it? If you're good at your job, you just want your boss to eliminate the obstacles and to help you do it better. If he's slow to respond or lacks whatever it takes to clear out any hindrances, who needs him? That's realism, folks. Yes, the management job is crucial to accomplishing work. But don't over glamorize it. "Help me or hurt me" is what we all care about.

So, then, what do leaders do?

Leaders inspire us to attain our highest achievements, and one way they do that is to create a vision of our work's importance – and of the special qualities of those people who do it well.

As I once explained to the Sales Execs who reported to me, "I bet you're doing better financially than most of your high school pals, aren't you? "They would nod. "And I bet you're doing better than most of your college pals, too." This time, they'd think about it, act a little surprised and then nod again. "There's a reason for that," I told them. "Not everyone can do what you do. You have to be intelligent. You have to be persuasive. You have to work your tail off every day. And...you have to be tough enough psychologically to handle frequent rejection. Few people can do all of that. And, please understand that without you, the economy simply would not move forward. You realize, right, that if every industrial salesperson in the country called in sick tomorrow that the entire U.S. economy would collapse? It's true, so be proud of what you do – it's hard, it's important, and very few people can do it as well as you."

Here's from **Cybersecurity** Security Executive Guido: "Using the Internet has become an integral part of life in the modern world. People, corporations, and governments are now totally reliant on it. From communicating to traveling to banking to commerce, nearly every aspect of our life revolves around the cyber world. At the same time, cybercriminals, corporate spies, rogue states, insiders and political campaigners have now the ability to remotely disrupt, destroy, steal or extort all of this overnight. As the number of cyber threats keeps rising exponentially and attacks become more complex, the only thing that stands in front of them is us – cybersecurity professionals.

Realize that you are part of an elite group that assembles the top experts in their fields. Being able to identify, protect, detect, respond and recover from cyberattacks requires not only the best minds around but also professionals who are held to the highest ethical standards. We must act honorably, justly, responsibly, and legally. What we do matters, it matters greatly... and YES! there are very few people that can do this and YOU are ONE OF THEM !!"

And here's one from my friend, Brian, a **Vendor Management** Executive: "Our job is crucial, because we reduce our company's financial risk by implementing contractual protections. And we do this by securing the right service levels at the best price. These vendor cost savings we negotiate drive our bottom line and make us a much more profitable and competitive company than we'd be otherwise. And not just anyone can do this gig. You have to be a THINKER...and...you have to be a PEOPLE PERSON. So, just a reminder, folks: what we do matters, and not every-one can do it."

Another way good leaders inspire us is to make work more fun.

Good managers can do that, too. You just have to think about it. Fun individual and group recognition events can pop out of your own head, or you can get input from your direct reports. More on the fun aspects of work later.

Good leaders also inspire us by helping us get more out of our team-mates.

How? They consciously pass on helpful hints by suggesting to Fred, for example, that he ask Mary about a new technique she uncovered for completing a task faster and with a lower error rate. Fred benefits and then pays Mary back a few weeks later by sharing an insight he's uncovered with her. The effective leader sets these positive aspects of our better natures in motion and helps create a positive and successful work environment for the entire team, department or business unit.

The point here is that effective leaders can have a major impact on individual performance and accelerate overall business results.

Starting to sound as if Management and Leadership overlap a bit?

You're not far off, and that's good. Let's take it a little deeper then. You can be a superior manager and an okay leader. You can be a superior leader and an okay manager. The goal is to be superior at both. You can do it, and they are reinforcing skills. If you're a good leader, picking up sharper management skills will enhance your followership. If you're a good manager, picking up keener leadership skills will boost team achievement.

CHAPTER 2

HOW EFFECTIVE MANAGERS BECOME BETTER LEADERS

If you're an effective manager, you are a respected expert at the tasks at hand. You understand how your organization works, and you are a good analyst and problem solver. You can state team and individual objectives clearly, and you can accurately measure performance in their pursuit. You work your tail off to get the job done. There is a better than even chance that you are highly organized, detail oriented and naturally good at time management. Your organization is fortunate to have you on board. So, why not leave it at that? Good managers don't grow on trees, right?

And, anyhow, maybe you think great leaders have to be charismatic. That doesn't hurt, but, look, you don't have to be slender and beautiful. You don't have to play a mean lead guitar. In fact, you don't have to change your personality one single bit. Keep on being your good management self, because becoming a better leader won't detract at all from your management chops. You will be adding some new behaviors, and these are motivational techniques that I promise you will be able to master. You want to be as effective as you can be, right? Mastering the motivational techniques that follow will allow you do just that by helping you get even higher performance from your team and by keeping your superior performers engaged and on board. You will still be a great manager, but now you'll be a great leader, too. Guaranteed. I've seen it happen time and time again when the understanding dawns that, by God, you **can** do both. Somebody had to teach me most of these techniques, and now I'll start passing them on to you.

Advancing Your Leadership Profile, Step 1: Think About Each Team Member Every Day

It's easy to pay attention to those of your reports who are doing something spectacularly positive and to those who are spectacularly screwing things up or require a lot of attention because they're new. That can make you neglect the rest – if not for an extended period, still for too long. To guard against this, put a weekly check sheet on your desk or laptop to ensure you're thinking about every member of your team every day. Prepare it Friday night or over the weekend. Over on the right hand side of the document or spreadsheet, make any notes about items that you should be discussing or following up with each individual in the coming week.

Week of March 6

X = Thought About   > = Spoke With or Emailed

Name	Mon	Tues	Wed	Thurs	Fri	NOTES
Mary	X	X	X	>		Vacation plans? Who's backing up?
Fred	>	X	X	X		Share new vendor report at next monthly meeting
Jake	X	X	>	X		HR issue solved? Need help from me?
Chelsea	X	>	X	X		Set up interview for new BU Controller slot
Brad	X	X	X	>		Need anything from me?
Roberta	>	X	X	>		What's causing cash flow drop-off? Temporary?

Nobody's going to be neglected if you use this simple format every day. Just be sure it's right under your nose on the desk or on your PC. And you don't have to speak with or email every individual every day – you've heard of micromanagement? Hey, I said I'd give you some simple motivational techniques that will advance your leadership profile. This one definitely works, and you don't have to be a rock star to demonstrate that you're a leader. You're just **being** one. By checking in regularly but not too often, you're demonstrating that their work matters and that you are there to help them. My friend CIO Chris does this with a spread sheet. Just be sure you do it consistently.

Advancing Your Leadership Step 2: Spend "Field Time" with Them

You can literally be in the field with them if they are in Sales, Consulting, Technical Support or anything else involving live calls on external or internal clients. If it's a newer employee, this can be highly instructive for you and her. And, of course, it shows direct support from you. If it's a senior and highly successful employee, it may be more instructive for you, and it still shows direct support. At the very least it will be flattering to her to know that you think she and her performance are important. I mean, what would it look like if you didn't spend time observing their work? Just be sure you take your instructions from your employee in these client visits beforehand regarding what she would like you to cover or to avoid. And even the most superior performers can benefit from having you along, because it lets her tell the client that she considers them important enough to introduce them to her boss, should they ever need any support in her absence. Clients appreciate that, as well they should.

So, how do you spend one-on-one time with them if you're in IT or Vendor Management or Finance, i.e., "the field" is inside? You may find it helpful to literally keep your door open whenever possible. That way, of course, they can access you when needed. Otherwise, you want to be sure to spend time with them at their desk or in a conference room to render support. This is not a Review and Plan or a monthly or quarterly Appraisal or feedback session we're talking about here. Those are important, too, and we'll discuss them later. This spending field time element of leadership is about getting to know the employee and her work and about providing relevant support to her and to other team members to advance individual and team performance. And that's a key element of what leaders do: provide direct and useful support. Naturally, you want to avoid overdoing it, lest you succumb to the sin of micromanagement. Because you never forget that your basic job is to help them vs. hurt them, right?

Advancing Your Leadership Profile Step 3: Manage Them One-on-One

You are managing a team of people, so you will hold live and remote team meetings, and you will regularly send out emails to the team as a whole. It's efficient, and everyone should be hearing the same thing on certain aspects of company requirements, market changes and performance updates. However, when you're starting out in management, you will definitely want to establish a personalized, one-off relationship with every individual who reports to you. My friend Steve became a Sales Manager on the East Coast at the same time I was becoming one on the West Coast. We were both in our mid-20s, pretty young for the position. He told me that right off the bat he didn't have the confidence to stand up in front of his team and call them to action. However, he knew he could handle them one-on-one, so he had a quick series of meetings with each team member. He offered to help each on a personal, customized basis. He did a fine job of it, such that the word started to spread among the team members that Steve was a pretty cool guy. And in short order he became the hub in the wheel with all of the members being the spokes. Then, when he stood up in front of the team, he was confident of securing their followership, because he had already earned their support as individuals. Worked like a charm.

And it's the best way to manage your direct reports even if you've worked with some of them for years. You will and should have a different relationship with each member based on their needs and yours. Sometimes, that's called Situational Management or Relationship vs. Task Management. If it's someone new, your stress will be on Task, because that emphasis is necessary to ensure the employee gets off on the right foot. As his performance improves, you will leverage your personal and professional Relationship with him to ensure his strongest performance. And if his performance falters, you start to emphasize Task again. Makes sense, right? Hey, people aren't all the same, so why manage them all the same?

Back to taking the team or Business Unit or entire company over when you're brand new to the assignment: that's the perfect time to ask a broad range of key people what advice they have for you. And be sure to do this high and low to get a good understanding of what **they** understand about the organization. You may find that people at the top think their communications are traveling all the way down with everyone getting the same message, and maybe they're not.

You can start each intro conversation by just flat out asking, "Hey, Marie, what advice do you have for me?" And then, of course, just shut up and listen. And here are the three standard questions to include in your conversation: START, STOP and CONTINUE. What should we start doing that we aren't doing now? What should we stop doing that we're doing now? What should we continue doing that we're doing now?

Another item when you're new: shuffling the team deck. You get a brief honeymoon period of about ninety days to assess the situation. People kind of expect that you'll make some personnel changes based on "fit" or "chemistry." If you wait much longer, then you may take some heat for removing someone who others think was doing well enough. And if you simultaneously leave an obvious loser in place, they'll wonder about your judgement, causing a lot of initial good will to evaporate. There's a very good book out on the broader take over topic, entitled The First 90 Days. [1] And don't forget, always managing your direct reports one-on-one will always make you a better leader - that's during the first ninety days and forever.

Advancing Your Leadership Profile Step 4: Vary Your Recognition Formats

Sure, team and BU emails to recognize stellar performances are just fine. And we all expect to hear about key achievements at the end of the month, quarter, half year and full year and at all team, departmental and company

---

[1] The First 90 Days by Michael D. Watkins, Harvard Business Review

meetings. There are other things you can do to celebrate and reward stellar performance, too – whether it's for a new methodology introduced advancing data accuracy in Finance or securing a new vendor who provides better performance at lower cost in the Sourcing Department. People do some truly remarkable things in business, and everybody enjoys their being recognized for it. Certainly, the hero who does something wonderful enjoys it. And so do her co-workers. Maybe she's a dog lover. So you can buy her a wooden plaque for home that says "Dogs Welcome / People Tolerated." Or a Dog Lover Adult Coloring Book. Okay, maybe it's dumb, but she'll laugh and so will her teammates. What's wrong with recognizing a winner and having a little fun for everybody? And it makes it memorable, too. That's part of your Leadership role, too: Making work more fun!

Here's one you can probably only use once: sending flowers and a congratulatory note to a female employee's husband or significant other. That's done with some frequency to wives or significant others of male performers. Nobody expects it the other way around, though, so you will get a laugh out of it and everybody will hear about it. It makes the recognition a bigger deal and gives it a longer life, as the story spreads. Hey, give it a shot. Nothing to lose. The point here is that mixing up your recognition moves keeps them fresh and meaningful to those recognized and to their co-workers.

If you're the boss, a dinner at a nice restaurant with the employee and his wife and with you and your husband or significant other is always a great recognition move. You all just get closer, and it often translates to better relationships and better performances at work. Three couples, if it makes sense and isn't forced, seems to work even better. Kind of a multiplier effect, but not too many people so it stays personal and fun. Plus, it dilutes the boss / employee aspect of the event in a positive, genuinely friendly way.

Advancing Your Leadership Profile Step 5: Perform High Quality, Thoughtful Appraisals

As a young Naval Officer fresh out of college, I had twenty even younger sailors reporting to me on the USS Cleveland (LPD-7). Our WESTPAC tours lasted nearly a year at sea. Twice a year, we officers would write up half page appraisals on each direct report. All I could think of was the sailors' concerned parents who might read them, so I wanted Mom and Pop, as well as the sailors themselves, to be able to recognize Malcolm or Jimmy in my description of their young stalwarts. I wrote something specific that each had done and referred to character and personality traits that had served them and the ship well. I don't know where that came from. I just know that I always considered it an important responsibility as a leader, and I still do.

A lot of annual appraisals in industry today are "check the box" documents in the view of the appraised – in part, because the employees have to complete them on themselves before giving them to their managers for review and signature just to satisfy an HR requirement. If you're the CEO of a company, kill that, will you? And if you're not, do your own genuine appraisals in addition to the required company documents. Will that be an extra workload for you? Yup, and it's worth every hour you invest, because you're proving that your team members and their performances matter to you, their leader, and to the company, too. The classical appraisal, which comments on Objective Performance and Skills and Functions, e.g., Planning & Organizing, Communications, Internal

Relationships, is the basic document here, and it works just fine. Essentially, it rates the employee on what she did and how she did it. Be as specific as you can in relating what the individual did well, using examples. If they're important, mention areas for improvement so that the employee can grow. Don't nit-pick, but don't shy from performing your duty to give straight feedback, either. And when describing these "challenges," be sure to make some specific suggestions on how the employee can achieve progress. In each category you appraise, you can use the traditional 1 – 5 system. One stinks, and a five means he walks on water. From top to bottom, it's Exceptional, Exceeds Expectations, Meets Expectations, Needs Improvement and Unsatisfactory.

This next recommendation I just stumbled on. Do you think Annual Appraisals should be written in the second or third person? Traditionally, it's been the third person (he or she did such-and-such). Maybe the goal was to achieve objectivity. Well, try doing it in the second person (*"you* achieved this, Marie"). I think I'm an honest guy most of the time, yet I found that saying "Jake, *you* created an extremely valuable check list for all of us," or "*your* inattention to detail sometimes causes others' problems, Joyce," forced even more honest feedback out of me somehow. And, of course, when you're sitting down with Marie, Jake and Joyce during their individual sessions, they will take your comments more personally, too.

You want to applaud their accomplishments during the reporting period, and you want to encourage them to make any truly necessary changes for the future. **Do the Appraisal process well, and you will stand out as one of the best leaders they ever had.**

Okay, what about feedback sessions other than the annual appraisal? Personally, I believe you should have a monthly

Review and Plan session with everyone reporting to you. It should last from thirty to sixty minutes and cite their performance for the month prior – both results and activities. How did they do vs. agreed upon expectations? Then, plan for the next month: what results and activities will they produce? What support is needed to make those results happen? Should you put this In writing? Yes. It can be as lengthy or as brief as you see fit, based on their performance and upcoming challenges.

Performance Appraisal and Development Plan

Employee
Name:_____

Job Title:
_____

Job Code:
_____

Org. Unit:
_____

Product Line/Dept. No:

Date of Evaluation:
_____

Period of Appraisal:
_____

(From _____)   (To _____)

Evaluating Manager:
_____

(Signature)

Reviewed By:
_____

(Signature of next level of management)

_____

Instructions:

Review Guidelines for Salaried/Exempt Employee Performance Appraisal and Development Planning for complete instructions. Manager may attach a list of current job duties and additional pages. Manager should complete all sections.

Section I: Appraise employee's performance by reviewing results achieved relative to objectives which were set at the beginning of the performance appraisal period.

Section II: Appraise skills and functions which relate to the way the employee accomplishes duties and performance objectives.

Section III: Discuss and set performance objectives for the next appraisal period.

Section IV: Describe plans for professional development which will help the employee achieve performance objectives, job duties, and career objectives.

I. Appraisal of Results Achieved (List most important objectives first. Circle appropriate performance ratings.)

Objective No. 1:

_____

28

_____

_____

Results Achieved:

_____

_____

_____

Unsatisfactory Needs Improvement Meets Expectations Exceeds Expectations
Exceptional

Objective No. 2:

_____

_____

_____

Results Achieved:

_____

_____

_____

Unsatisfactory Needs Improvement Meets Expectations Exceeds Expectations
Exceptional

Objective No. 3:

_____

_____

_____

Results Achieved:

_____

_____

_____

Unsatisfactory Needs Improvement Meets Expectations Exceeds Expectations
Exceptional

Objective No. 4:

_____

_____

_____

Results Achieved:

_____

_____

_____

**Unsatisfactory   Needs Improvement   Meets Expectations   Exceeds Expectations
Exceptional**

Unplanned Achievements/Other Activities:
_____

_____

_____

**Unsatisfactory   Needs Improvement   Meets Expectations   Exceeds Expectations
Exceptional**

II. Appraisal of Performance Skills & Functions

Quanity of Work:
_____

_____

_____

**Unsatisfactory   Needs Improvement   Meets Expectations   Exceeds Expectations
Exceptional**

Quality of Work:
_____

_____

_____

**Unsatisfactory   Needs Improvement   Meets Expectations   Exceeds Expectations
Exceptional**

Technical Competence or Job Knowledge:
_____

_____

_____

**Unsatisfactory   Needs Improvement   Meets Expectations   Exceeds Expectations
Exceptional**

Teamwork: What working relationship has the individual established with fellow employees in the working environment?

_____

_____

_____

**Unsatisfactory   Needs Improvement   Meets Expectations   Exceeds Expectations
Exceptional**

Planning and Organizing: Are assignments approached in an organized fashion? Is there an appreciation of planning activities?

_____

_____

_____

**Unsatisfactory   Needs Improvement   Meets Expectations   Exceeds Expectations
Exceptional**

Communication: Can this individual communicate clearly and concisely with managers, peers, subordinates, and customers? How good is written and oral communication?

_____

_____

_____

**Unsatisfactory   Needs Improvement   Meets Expectations   Exceeds Expectations
Exceptional**

Development of Others: Can this person give effective assistance to others when needed? As a manager or supervisor does this person effectively develop subordinates?

_____

_____

_____

**Unsatisfactory   Needs Improvement   Meets Expectations   Exceeds Expectations
Exceptional**

Overall Performance Appraisal: Circle the rating which best summarizes the employees overall performance. Explain the rating below.

**Unsatisfactory   Needs Improvement   Meets Expectations   Exceeds Expectations
Exceptional**

Explanation

_____

_____

_____

I. Performance Objectives for Next Appraisal Period

(From _____ To _____

Objective No. 1:

_____

_____

_____

Objective No. 2:

_____

_____

_____

Objective No. 3:

_____

_____

Objective No. 4:

_____

_____

_____

Safety Objective:

_____

_____

_____

Affirmative Objective:

_____

_____

I. Plans for Professional Development

_____

_____

_____

_____

Employee Review of the Performance Appraisal and Development Plan (Required)

I have reviewed this form and discussed the contents with my manager. My signature means that I have been advised of my performance and does not necessarily imply that I agree with the appraisal or the ratings.

Employee Signature: Date:

_____   _____

Employee's Comments (Optional)

Any comments the employee wishes to make concerning the appraisal may be written here. Additional comments may be attached on a separate piece of paper. Employee may discuss comments with next level of management.

Employee should sign the completed form and be provided with a copy.

Download this form at: http://growthaccelerators.com/book

Advancing Your Leadership Profile Step 6: Delegate Administrative Tasks to an Administrator

Hire a smart, organized and pleasant administrator. If you don't have access to somebody to support you and your team, do everything in your power to get one. A sharp administrator can get so much done effectively and efficiently across lines and up and down your organization. If well trained and well directed by you, she will be a major business performance accelerator for you and the organization.

 When I was a first-line manager, I didn't want to be associated with minutia. I just wanted them to think that all Jack cares about is revenue and net additions to the population. Period. So...I put our superior Administrator, Carol, 100% in charge of Expense Reports, even though that was my responsibility. She did a better job of it than I would have, and I didn't have to dilute my focus on the more crucial performance objectives. Now, Carol was a leader, and the best Administrators usually are. They're also smart enough to win everyone's respect so that things they're in charge of get done right and on time. It's like any other position: there are also-rans and superstars. When my business partner and I started our first company, any Executive Assistant reporting to us who turned out to be a superstar we transferred to the Sales Department. Why? Because our company wouldn't go anywhere if we didn't have a highly productive Sales Department, right? We did this about three times while settling, ourselves, for the occasional average performer. Finally, we grew big enough and profitable enough that we told our CFO to hire an ace just for us whom we would keep. She complied and found Chris for us. Chris commanded a higher salary, based on her prior experience and skill level. She was worth every penny. Many years later, she is still a good friend to my partner and me while now providing her professional services to a company in another state.

Advancing Your Leadership Profile Step 7: Make Your Team Meetings Useful vs. Mandatory

As they in show biz, you always open with a strong act, and you close with a strong act. If you're going to a Stones concert, are they going to open with "Angie?" No. Not a bad song, but they're going to open with "Brown Sugar" or "Honky-Tonk Woman" or another one that gets you up on your feet screaming and shouting. Same thing with their last number. It'll be "Paint It Black," "Gimme Shelter" or "Satisfaction." A former Administrator, Helen, told me that she and her husband always ensured the success of their dinner parties by doing a big "HELLO" to every couple when they arrived and a big "GOODBYE" when they left. "Oh, come on in, George and Molly! Fred and I are so glad you could make it." And at the end, "Thanks so much for coming, guys! It's always a great party when you join us, George and Molly!" Let the middle take care of itself.

The best way to open and close any team or company meeting is with Recognition. It's positive, and it's fun. You can also open with humor. If you're a great comedian, go for it. I'm not, so I often open with a cartoon that I've plucked from The New Yorker or elsewhere. Just pass them out or flash them up on the screen. The whole point here is to make your meetings fun as well as instructive. And that makes you come across as a leader, someone fun to work for.

Always pass out an agenda beforehand or just after your joke or Recognition announcements. People like to know where the meeting is headed and whether or not their immediate concerns are being addressed. If they aren't on the agenda, they can ask you on the spot if you'll consider opening their topic for discussion. If not, you can just make plans to meet afterwards.

What your team enjoys the most is their own participation. If each gets up to present their plans for the upcoming quarter, they will absolutely LOVE your meeting. And you can always designate in advance a 15 to 30-minute presentation from one or two of them on a topic of interest to everyone on the team, e.g., a new federal accounting rule, a new product offering, a new personnel policy.

You can also invite internal and external clients to present on occasion for useful insights and good entertainment. HR Managers are often enlightening speakers. And as important as it is to have fun at your meetings, it's more important that your team members find them useful, advancing their ability to do their job better. Goes back to help me or hurt me, right? And if you're recognized as being a manager who consistently throws a good meeting, be it weekly monthly, quarterly or annually, you will also be recognized as being a good leader, too.

Advancing Your Leadership Profile Step 8: Toastmasters

Depending on your public speaking experience, you may find this an unnecessary step or one of the most useful "leadership builders" on the planet. Next to AA, I think this program has the highest success rate around. I confess I haven't exploited it myself; however, I've got a ton of friends who swear by it. I didn't do it because I've played in a semi-pro rock band, given tons of speeches in student government and business roles and called my department to order on deck every day in the Navy for two years. It's easy for me to get up in front of a small group or a large one, because I've done it so many times. However, if you haven't, then do check out Toastmasters, either at your company, in your neighborhood or in the city where you work. They're all over the place. What they do is give you the opportunity to get up and speak to others so often that you get very used to it. And not only does this make you a better public speaker, it advances your leadership confidence across the board. Trust me: you'll be pleasantly surprised at how well this works. It's not that you lack public speaking skills – you just haven't done it enough to master it. And if you are a manager in charge of developing other managers or management candidates, be sure to include a discussion of Toastmasters. Again, it's such an easy fix, a perfect example of how it's easier to change behavior than to change attitudes.

Advance Your Leadership Profile Step 9: Develop Your Management Candidates

I can remember how I loved managing my friend TK when he was a new Sales Manager reporting to me, his Branch Manager. TK would just rave over the answers I'd give when he's ask me how to do things. One day, on a hunch, I said, "What do you think, TK?" Well, guess what? His answer was better than the one I had in mind. I never forgot that lesson. Sure, all employees need close attention when they're new. It's part of a standard Situational Management approach. Just don't keep it up too long, because you'll both get used to operating that way, potentially limiting the employee's growth. What if TK had given me the wrong answer? Try this: "Sounds good, TK; however, you need to look out for such and such." Or, "Perfect, but shave it here and here – know why, TK?" Keep it a learning experience by continuing to ask questions without being a pain.

You can occasionally develop two of your direct reports simultaneously by suggesting to Charlie that he consult Emelia who recently faced the same challenge and came up with a positive solution. Tell him to check back in with you afterwards. Emelia will grow by gathering her thoughts and helping her teammate, and it will advance her self-confidence. She'll also be flattered that you told her peer that she did something so well – excellent recognition! And if that brings her and Charlie closer, they may start trading tips which will advance both their business performances.

Now, please know that even your best direct reports will have weaknesses. Not to worry. As premier management consultant and college professor Peter Drucker pointed out in The Effective Executive[2] a few years ago, we should hire people for their strengths. Don't worry about their weaknesses unless they undermine the very strengths you hired them for. Example: an inspiring, charismatic leader who stinks at follow-up. That weakness can hurt performance, especially after he raises our hopes so high. So...you do need to neutralize that weakness, get him up to average or better in terms of responsiveness. More on that in a later section.

On a related item, what should you do when you don't know the answer? You've asked your friends, your peers, your boss,

---

[2] The Effective Executive by Peter Drucker, HarperCollins

your direct reports – everyone – and you're still struggling. Don't despair. Rejoice, because you may be on the verge of an epiphany, an intellectual breakthrough. That is how our minds work. Synapses firing in our brains for a few days or weeks, even, as we struggle to come up with the magic solution.

Of course, there's nothing magic about it. "Struggle and insight go together," says David Perkins, research professor at the Harvard Graduate School of Education. "You are not likely to achieve an insight, unless you've struggled with the problem some."

If you are specifically developing someone for a management role, it is wise to have a list of requirements that both of you can examine for current proficiency and for progress if the item is important enough.

SELF DEVELOPMENT ANALYSIS

NAME:

_____

DATE:

_____

Below are listed a number of skills, traits and factors, considered important to job effectiveness. Rate yourself as you think you really are. You may want to have other co-workers rate you as they see you.

PART A. INDIVIDUAL PERSONALITY CHARACTERISTICS

1. HUMAN RELATIONS SKILL

Overall ability to deal smoothly and effectively with people at all levels

Needs Improvement	Average for company personnel	Unusually skilled
Remarks:		

2. INITIATIVE

Need to excel; having high personal standards of accomplishment

Tends to follow precedent	Has necessary drive - does a good job	Need to excel is unusually high
Remarks:		

3. INSPIRATION TO OTHERS

Is the kind of person that others admire and want to copy

Not likely to inspire others	Average in inspiring others	Very skilled in inspiring others
Remarks:		

4. THOROUGHNESS AND SELF-RELIANCE IN PROBLEM SOLVING

Resourcefulness and personal involvement in the many details of a problem

Tends to overlook important elements	Meets standards on job	Exceptionally thorough
Remarks:		

40

5. INSIGHT INTO SELF

Understands weaknesses and strong points and can discuss them with objectivity	Needs self-insight	Average self-understanding	Knows self very well
Remarks:		

6. CONTINUAL SELF-DEVELOPMENT

Degree to which one continuously works at self-improvement	Tends to rest on laurels	Intermittent application	Practically always is working to develop self
Remarks:		

7. SEEKS NEW RESPONSIBLITIES

Enjoys the challenge of new and heavy responsibility	Does not want heavy responsibility	Will accept a heavy responsibility when asked	Continually reaches out for new responsibilities
Remarks:		

8. MENTAL CAPACITY

Reasoning ability, speed in learning new ideas and general understanding	Below average for most people in his/her position	Good-sufficient for present responsibilities	Very high--brighter then most in his/her position
Remarks:		

9. EMOTIONAL MATURITY

Objectivity, self-control, appropriateness of behavior to all situations	Whines, blames others, lowers group morale	Adequate	Deals successfully with setbacks, solution oriented
Remarks:		

10. ADAPTABILITY TO NEW CONDITIONS

Ability to adjust readily to new and unforeseen circumstances	Slow to adapt to new conditions	Average in flexibility	Can handle new situations with relative ease
Remarks:		

11. PERSISTENCE

Ability to continue working toward a goal even though success or rewards appear to be far into the future	Improvement needed	Adequate to job demands	Outstanding
Remarks:		

12. INTEGRITY

Honest and forthcoming, sound business ethics	Covers up, bends company policies	Generally acceptable business ethics	Uncompromising professional integrity
	Remarks:		

PART B. JOB SKILLS

13. VOLUME OF WORK

Quantity of acceptable work	Should be increased	Regularly meets standards	Usually high output
	Remarks:		

14. QUALITY

Thoroughness, accuracy, neatness of work	Improvement needed	Regularly meets standards	Consistently meets highest standards
	Remarks:		

15. PLANNING, ORGANIZING AND SCHEDULING WORK

Skill in quickly and efficiently organizing, planning and scheduling work.	Improvement needed	Adequate to job demands	outstanding-very good in planning and coordinating work
	Remarks:		

16. FOLLOWING UP ON SUBORDINATES

(For Managers) Ability to smoothly follow-up on work of subordinates without their feeling overly supervised	Improvement needed-- to much faith in subordinates	Adequate	Takes nothing for granted - skilled in keeping informed without being "bossy"
	Remarks:		

17. COST CONSCIOUSNESS

influence of cost and profit considerations in decisions and judgments	Tends to overlook cost factors	Average	Very high
	Remarks:		

18. METHODS IMPROVEMENT

Ability to devise new methods to achieve business objectives	Improvement needed	Adequate to job demands	Very high - can cite many examples of new methods
	Remarks:		

42

19. COMPANY PERSPECTIVE			
Has attitude and insight into matters affecting both departmental and company welfare	Improvement needed	Sufficient for present assignment	Very broad perspective
Remarks:			

20. JOB KNOWLEDGE			
Breadth of factual knowledge, technical and nontechnical, related to job	Needs more knowledge	Has required knowledge	Has thorough knowledge of own and related work
Remarks:			

21. VERBAL SKILLS			
Ability to talk easily and clearly in all situations	Improvement needed	Adequate to job demands	Well above average in verbal skill - enjoys talking
Remarks:			

22. WRITING SKILLS			
Ability to write with clarity, brevity and reader interest	Improvement needed	Adequate to job demands	Well above average
Remarks:			

23. OVER-ALL PERFORMANCE			
Considering all the above factors	Barely acceptable performance	Good performance but not outstanding	Outstanding
Remarks:			

Download this form at: http://growthaccelerators.com/book

You should fill this out on her, and the person you're developing should fill one out on herself. If you or she desire to get anonymous or acknowledged feedback from teammates and others, you certainly may do that. Not strictly necessary, however, in my experience. If one or two of these items represents a serious need for improvement, i.e., a serious weakness, then you should consider using the attachment below to focus in on these – one characteristic per page.

Facilitating Coaching and Development Discussion
Personal Development Plan

After a coaching and development conversation has occurred, personal development plan should be created for the 1-3 areas of opportunity that have been identified. Use the worksheet below to guide the development of an action plan to address each area of opportunity.

AREA FOR DEVELOPMENT	
CURRENT BEHAVIOR/KNOWLEDGE/SKILLS	DESIRED BEHAVIOR/KNOWLEDGE/SKILLS
ACTIONS (WHAT SPECIFIC ACTIONS MUST BE TAKEN?)	
BENEFITS (WHAT ARE THE BENEFITS TO YOU AND THE ORGANIZATION?)	BARRIERS (WHAT STANDS IN YOUR WAY?)
REQUESTS/RESOURCES (WHAT TRAINING OR SUPPORT DO YOU NEED?)	TIMELINE (WHAT MILESTONES DO YOU NEED TO MEET BY WHEN?)
ACHIEVEMENT METRICS (WHAT ARE KEY SUCCESS METRICS TO DEMONSTRATE PROGRESS, QUALITATIVE AND/OR QUANTATIVE?)	

Download this form at: http://growthaccelerators.com/book

Advancing Leadership Profile Step 10: Welcome Intellectual Conflict

Want the best solution for your team, business or organization? Of course, you do. So...let the folks argue about it – including you. Just don't make it personal, what we call an ad hominem argument. The best way to keep on pressing your point if you strongly feel you're right is to apologize after a bit, stressing that you're not pushing this to be a jerk but that you honestly think this is the best way to go and that you are gladly willing to be dissuaded by a better argument. Otherwise, tell them, you'll feel like a wuss if you backed off too soon and that you wouldn't be doing your best for the team.

I always thought I was a pretty gutsy guy unafraid to put my opinions out there until one of my bosses, Jim, gave me feedback that I was shying away from conflict. Me??!!? "Yeah, you, Jack." He brought up an example from a recent staff meeting. I thought about it hard and decided that sometimes I just like to bring the group together and move on. Jim's point was that I was compromising too early for the good of the team, prematurely cutting off healthy argument that could lead to a better solution. Sold.

Another time, boss Bill told me and the other three senior departmental managers reporting to him that it was his job, not ours, to make final compromises and that we should each push our individual department's objectives and concerns hard so he could understand all of the implications, positive and negative, of his upcoming decision. I ran Sales, and the other VPs ran Tech, Finance and HR. We all got along and were sensitive to each other's challenges and that was great for everyday operations. In fact, it was necessary for a well-oiled team to work that way. However, Bill was right. It was his job to make the final call on policy decisions after weighing the total impact on all elements of our business. And that doesn't mean we couldn't argue with him, i.e., engage in intellectual conflict, if we didn't like his final call. It meant that we should be blunt in our assessments of the impact of the decision on our departments. That was good for everybody, because it would enhance our ability to come up with the best policy in the end.

Yes, we should welcome intellectual conflict, even knowing that it can get out of hand sometimes. Again, if you find yourself getting too harsh, stop yourself and apologize – and then keep on! In the end, you'll be helping to identify the best decision available. Sometimes, progress just don't come easy, ya' know?

LEADERSHIP EXTRAS

What Is the Value of Public Criticism?

None, absolutely none. Isn't it nice to have some black and white rules? The only time you see some fool do this occurs when that guy who thinks he should be the boss because he's smarter than everybody else decides to assert himself. So, just because you see some idiots still adopting this behavior, don't even think about doing it yourself.

How to Communicate Bad News and Good News

This is kind of fun. With bad news, you do have to communicate it so people can plan around it. To the extent possible, however, you want to contain its impact. And the best way to do that is to slip it out there in advance so that when it hits, it's already been discounted. When I was managing a 110-man corporate branch in Alaska, I had to communicate the Cost of living Allowance (COLA) twice per year. It was about 40% compared to the lower 48 as a composite and was based on the Consumer Price Index. One year I had to communicate that it was going to be flat after our national headquarters gave me the word. I knew that wouldn't make the troops happy, especially since I had to announce it in winter when things are kind of unpleasant across the board up there due to the absence of sun most of the day. The murder rate goes up along with the suicide rate. The Field Technicians want to unionize, and the Sales Reps don't want to sell anything. I was sitting in my office trying to figure out how I should handle this when I saw a friend of mine, Fritz, outside my door in the Administrative area. "Hey, Fritz, come on in! How you doing, man? I heard you got a new dog. Take him hunting yet? Hey, don't tell a soul, but I've got to send out a memo on Friday telling the whole branch that the COLA is going to be flat this time. Damn. Oh, well, good to see you, man. Take care." Naturally, Fritz immediately went and blabbed it to a couple of folks who each told a couple more and so on. By the time I sent out the memo on Friday, all you heard was, "Yeah, yeah, that sucks... those dumb headquarters economists, what do they know?" Trust me, it could have been a lot worse. It's much like the Federal Reserve Board Chair hinting they might be buying bonds to raise the interest rate. When it's finally made official, the stock market takes it largely in stride; because the news isn't shattering. It's already been hinted at in advance - get it?

Now, with good news, it's just the opposite. Don't tell a soul until you're ready to explode the news to the whole group at once. Back to Alaska. Headquarters told us Branch Managers in a private memorandum that in Q4, any Sales Rep who achieved 125% of quota would receive a $10,000 bonus. I didn't tell anyone. In late September, I called in the outlying Reps and got the full Sales Force in our Demo Room for a new product training session. At the end, I said, "And here's some news you might like: anyone who achieves 125% of plan in Q4 GETS A TEN THOUSAND DOLLAR BONUS!!!" They went wild, screaming and shouting, jumping up and down. It echoed off the walls, and the administrators told me you could hear the shouts out on the street as they were leaving for home.

Laura, a friend of mine, was a Sales Manager in the first company I started a few years later. She adapted my advice to the management of her two young sons. If she had told them the family was going to Disneyland here in Southern California and then learned it wouldn't happen because her husband was getting called out of town on business, she would tell one of them early in the week, "Ooh, Scotty, it's starting to look shaky on Disneyland this Saturday. Daddy might be called away on business. Okay, honey, be a good boy in school today – and have fun, too!" Of course, Scott would tell brother Matt. Then, Friday night when they were sitting around the dinner table, she'd say "Boys, I'm sorry to tell you..." Before she could finish, they'd both say, "Yeah, yeah, we know, no Disneyland tomorrow." A lot better than shedding tears and screaming, true? On the other hand, when she and her husband knew they were going to be able to take them to Disneyland, Laura wouldn't say a word until they were all sitting around eating their ham and eggs on Saturday morning. Then, she'd slap both hands on the table. "Hey, I know, let's just all get in the car and go to Disneyland!" Yup, you needed ear plugs with both boys shouting for joy.

When Your Top Performer Says She's Joining Your Competitor

Ugh. But it happens, doesn't it? Another corporate Branch Manager pal, Dave A., taught me how to handle this one. Yes, I'll admit that sometimes when a top gun would tell me she's leaving to join our competitor, I'd lose it and say something like, "That's crazy, Jill! We're much better than they are. Why would you ever want to do that?!!?" Then, I'd walk away while Jill, of course, became more convinced than ever that she made the right move.

Okay, here's a better way to proceed. Stay calm and express your sadness that she's departing. And tell her how lucky you and the firm were to have benefitted from her superior performance. All true, right? She did contribute greatly and you are genuinely sad to be losing her. Now...tell her you'd like to take her to lunch on Friday to the best place in town to thank her for her contribution and to wish her well. Have a good time at lunch discussing family, upcoming vacations, etc. And then, as you're wrapping up, thank her once more for her great contribution. Finally, say this, "Jill, I hope your new relationship works out, but we all know that sometimes the gig turns out to be less than we expected – not because anyone was dishonest – it just happens. So, if that should occur, please know that we would welcome you back with open arms. I wouldn't want you to feel embarrassed to call me. We'd throw a ticker tape parade if you returned! I'm going to check your re-hire box twice, Jill. So good luck, friend, and please stay in touch."

I found that half the time after this Friday lunch the highly valued employee would come in and tell me on Monday that she'd decided to stay, that she hadn't realized how much she was valued by me and by the firm. Does that indicate we weren't doing a great job in the recognition arena? Well.... yes. Resolve to do better. Many other times, usually within a year after she left us, the individual would return, because I'd given her the strong signal that we would rejoice at our good fortune, which, of course, we did.

CHAPTER 3

HOW DO NATURAL LEADERS BECOME

BETTER MANAGERS?

Ever notice that some "natural leaders" stink at follow-through? That hurts us doubly because they raise our hopes so high before letting us down. If you're one of those (and I think I was early on), we've got to correct that weakness and move it up to acceptable standards. We've got to get you organized and quick at follow-through for your direct reports, your associates and your boss. Help Me / Hurt Me, right?

Someone can be a leader in business or social settings or the military or sports or religion or hobby groups or politics, to name a few arenas. Does this leadership ability translate from one arena to another? Of course, it does, because you either got it or you don't, right? Bzzzt! WRONG. In fact, with all the literature on Leadership out there, psychologists still don't understand why some people have plenty of it and some have less. Here's an obvious example: if someone is the legitimate and well-respected leader at work, will he be the captain of the intra-company softball team if he's not much of a jock and someone else is a former major leaguer and a nice guy, to boot? No, we'd rather go with the pro.

Here's an example describing who the social leaders are at the Fortune 100 company where I worked for thirteen years before striking out on my own. In both the Bay Area and here in SoCal, we have frequent reunions of the folks who worked at this fine organization some years back. Well, I was one of the business leaders in SoCal, and there are others. However, it's Gary, who was a Sales Rep and who now lives in Hawaii who organizes this event. He loves doing it, he's creative and he delivers! Same thing in the Bay Area. John was a high-powered National Account Manager (very senior Sales Rep). He organizes every detail and films it with interviews of the attendees, and I can't wait to see it every year. Neither cared to be a business leader. Unquestionably, they are both superior social leaders. And lucky for the rest of us that they are.

Personally, it's a lot easier for me to lead if I have respect for those I'm leading. It makes me want to do my absolute best for them. Can I lead the members of my Homeowners Association? Well.... no.

Now, we already know that some natural leaders will not be so hot at management. Not to worry, natural leaders. You don't have to change who you are to become better managers. You do have to expand your skills repertoire, however, or you will be far less successful than you should be.

Advancing Your Management Profile Step 1: Organize Yourself

Before we were married, my wife, who worked at the same company, helped me with this when I was promoted to Sales Manager. "Gail, I know I can lead these folks. I respect them, I hired several of them and I can make it fun around here while banging the numbers. But I don't have a clue about getting myself organized." She was a former school teacher and then a customer trainer, and she told me to sit down at my desk.

First, she had me place an 8 ½ x 11 pad on the right side of my desk and list all my "A" priorities. Then, she had me place the relevant paperwork for those priorities in a folder on the left side of my desk. Behind me in a drawer were files with every Sales Rep's name where I could put notes about positive achievements, "challenge" areas and anything else relevant to supporting and managing that Rep. I also had a large calendar right behind my desk that showed every month on two 8 ½ x 11 inch sheets. I could record appointments and look at every day, week and month - current, past and forward. It all worked! Simple, yes – but it was absolutely good enough to keep me on track. I still use the big pad on the right side of my desk to list my "A" priorities, and I still use a big paper calendar. On my laptop are the folders I need to attack those priorities (My Docs), and I have a folder for every client and / or employee for whom I'm responsible. Yes, I am still not the most organized guy around, but it is no longer a weakness – I am good enough. Phew!

So, make sure you find someone like Gail at work who's good at organization to help you. Someone at work is best, because he or she will understand the company, the culture and enough about your role to give you highly specific tutoring.

I almost forgot – here's one my business partner Tom taught me years ago when we were both Branch Managers at our Fortune 100 tech company. After church on Sunday, go into the office and get yourself set up for Monday. Clean out your emails, respond to any requests from national or regional management, send out any necessary emails to your branch employees and either tackle head-on or prepare to tackle any newly discovered challenges during the next week. In other words, set yourself up to manage and lead on Monday vs. coming in and getting set back on your heels. You can do it

Friday night, Saturday or Sunday. I have one friend, Guido, who comes in at 4:00 A.M. on Monday to set himself up. Whatever. Just ensure you're ready to lead the charge on Monday at 8:00 A.M.

Advance Your Management Profile Step 2: Follow Up on Team Members' Requests Instantly

Hey, you're going to have to do it anyhow, right? Why not do it immediately so your employee can back to doing her job right away? Celebrated business authors advise us to distinguish between the Urgent and the Important. And they're right. We can't just sit at our desktop and respond to every email that pops up. We've got to take plenty of time out for business planning, for example, because that's Important. However, when one of your aces needs your support, that really is Important as well as Urgent. And this is something that natural leaders frequently fail to respond to adequately. My good pal, Jimmy, and I were Sales Execs some years ago at a tech research firm and were good friends with another Sales Exec whom we'll call Mark. Cool guy, funny, loyal and helpful. Then he was promoted to Sales Manager, transferring from the West to the East Coast. A couple of years later, he transferred back and became Jimmy's and my direct manager. We were overjoyed. "Yay, Mark's back as the boss man! Nothing but good times ahead for us!" Well.... that's until we found out that Mark took two days to get back to us on everything, from negligible items to crucial ones. Not just for Jimmy and me. For everyone on the team. After about nine months, Mark was asked to step down, so he left to sell for another firm. Don't let this happen to you, natural leader.

My business partner Tom and I were co-CEOs in a couple of tech firms we started, and we shared a large office together at our various headquarters locations during a twenty-year period. It was very efficient, and we got a lot done that way while fully exploiting the "two heads are better than one" cliché to come up with good ideas we could implement quickly. Our door was always open. And even though our CFO, CIO, VP of Technical Service and a couple of Sales Managers operated out of our headquarters office, it was perfectly okay for anyone to come in and ask us for help if his boss wasn't available.

I remember the time Account Exec Joanne knocked on the door and peered in to ask for our assistance. I waved her in and told her to sit down. "What's up, Joanne?" "Hi, Jack. I think I can score at XYZ (a Fortune 500 company), but we need to ship and install the hardware next Wednesday. And I just heard that we're really tight on those devices. Can you help?" "Okay, Joanne, let me call the OEM headquarters right now." Then I picked up the phone and asked for Bill Mitchell, the head of the Western Region. "Yes, this is Jack Finnell, President of Ameritech Communications. May I speak with Mr. Mitchell, please? That's okay, I'll wait as long as it takes. This is crucial." Finally, Bill came on, and I said, "Yo, Bill, how you doing? Yeah, I'm good, too. Hey, I'm sitting here with my superstar Joanne who says we can kick out the competition at XYZ and place five high end units...BUT...we have to be able to deliver by next Wednesday, which means I'd need them in my warehouse by Tuesday morning at the latest. I hear those units are really scarce at this point in the month, so can you bail us out here, Bill?" Waiting.... waiting....waiting. "You can?!!? Oh, thanks, man! Yeah, I owe you one, Bill, and we will deliver. Thanks again, pard." Well, yes, of course Joanne is sitting there looking stunned that I pulled it off and did it so quickly. Was that hard?

Certainly not, and if I didn't do it then, I would have had to do it later, so why not do it instantly and get Joanne back to her prospect? After Joanne left, my partner Tom couldn't stifle his laugh. "You jackass, you did it again." He knew I loved the whole drama, and it was fun is the truth.

Now, did Joanne appreciate that professionally or personally? You're right: both. This is an action speaks louder than words thing. And, of course, it spurs even greater performance from the person you supported so instantly. And, of course, you never bring it up in the future, as in, "Now, Joanne, remember that time I intervened to get you that high end gear for XYZ corporation." Not classy – and not at all necessary. Although I list this as a Management Advancement Step, it secures your Leadership mandate, too. It is the epitome of Help Me / Hurt Me.

Advance Your Management Profile Step 3: Use PIP (Performance Improvement Plans) Wisely

If someone isn't suited for the job he's in and no amount of training or support will change that, then you have an obligation to him, to his teammates and to your organization to make the necessary change. Sometimes it's easy to know that someone should leave, and sometimes it's not. We'll discuss all of these situations. This is extremely important part of effective Management, by the way, so we're going to spend a good amount of time on this.

I'm not talking about something obvious that will get someone fired like sexual harassment or embezzlement. There are other times that you're sure, however, that this isn't the right gig for the individual. You've spent enough time observing and working directly with this person to know this is a bad fit. And I have to say I don't think I've ever seen anyone fired too early. It's human nature, perhaps, to bend over backwards to be actually certain that this isn't going to work out for the individual. So, if this is one of those times you're sure, you can either attempt to persuade him to leave now to look for employment for which he'd be better suited...or...you can take him straight to PIP.

It's best to have the Voluntary Separation discussion in your office at 3:00 on a Friday afternoon. Of course, you let him know earlier in the week. If he asks what the meeting is about, you tell him the truth: "It's about your performance." At your meeting you point out that his performance has been below standard for some time. If you've been doing monthly Review and Plan sessions, this comes as no surprise. To help salvage his pride, you tell him that you've been there yourself in a past endeavor. "Look, we both know you're smart. We both know you're a good person. And I've been in a similar situation myself. It was phone sales for a newspaper. I wasn't doing very well at it, and I didn't really like the job. It was circular, I guess. Anyhow, thank God I quit and found something better suited to my strengths and my interests. That's where I see you right now. Why stay in a job that can't be much fun nor a good opportunity for you to shine? Now, it's the middle of the month. You might want to think about this over the weekend, and if you decide to resign on Monday, effective October 31, you could start to look for a new job ASAP. I'll cover you for those two weeks. And be advised that you have every right to go through the 30-60-90 day PIP. You may decide, though, that it's in your interest to leave now. So, I'll see you back here at 8:00 on Monday when you can tell me your decision."

Well, of course, he goes home and has one of the most miserable weekends of his life. In the meantime, in preparation for your 8:00 Monday meeting, you have a Resignation Letter typed up from him to you, specifying that he will be leaving the organization on October 31 to pursue new opportunities. Keep it simple. Then, for legal reasons, have a letter typed from you to him formally accepting his resignation. Why? Just that if he changes his mind a couple of days later, you can say you're sorry but that the firm has decided that it's in their best interest that he leave. It's legal protection, if needed. I've never had that happen, but it's a good safeguard. By the way, I did have a phone sales gig schlepping newspapers. I was fourteen years old, put on my jacket and tie and took the train to the city on a fine summer's day and banged the phone all day long at the publisher's headquarters. Didn't close a single sale. Meanwhile, this crusty old guy next to me sat in his t-shirt smoking cigarettes and convinced a ton of people to sign up. So, I quit and went back to what I knew I could do well – delivering newspapers on my bike in the hood. Oh well...maybe it taught me some humility. Maybe.

If you're not sure if you should take someone out, there are a couple of things you can do. One of my favorite business books of all time is Analyzing Performance Problems[3] by Robert Mager and Peter Pipe. It's brief and to the point and oh so useful. It helps you justify your decision calmly, analytically and honorably. It includes a series of decision trees to guide you. Often, we cop out consciously or unconsciously and conclude that "he just needs more training." Well, perhaps. Or not, and this book will guide you. One of my favorite decision tree questions is, "Could he do it if his life depended on it?" If

---

[3] Analyzing Performance Problems by Mager & Pipe, Lake Publishing

the answer is "no," then let's find something else for him to do, either inside or outside our organization.

Quite recently, Steve, a friend of mine, took over national sales responsibility for a large Pharma company. He had an inkling that some of his direct reports should be reassigned and wanted advice on how to pull it off quickly and fairly. I steered him to the book, and it worked perfectly. And here's one of the chief benefits: since he was new, it not only helped him justify his final decisions in his own head and heart, it helped him convince his boss and his HR department that he was doing the right thing. He showed them the book and the relevant decision trees. Open and shut.

If you're really not sure whether the individual can or will perform at an acceptable level, then placing him on PIP can bring you the answer. When I was running that corporate Branch in Alaska, one of the Field Service Managers, Ed, seemed to be a pretty sharp guy, but he wasn't "into it" in my view. Low energy on the job, even though he was intelligent and had a good sense of humor. Submissions were late, and sometimes he was, too. No drug or alcohol issues, just kind of lackadaisical. So, I asked his boss, Mick, who reported to me what he thought.

He wasn't sure, either, even though he had told Ed repeatedly to show some more spark. So, I suggested putting him on PIP. Worked like a charm and rather quickly, too. Ed thanked us and said that was just what he needed to fire himself up. I've also had instances when people placed on PIP said, "Hey, maybe I should find something else to do. I'm getting kind of burned out in this gig."

Now, let's go to the individual who definitely should be taken out and who won't do so voluntarily, even after you tried the late Friday Voluntary Separation discussion. In this instance, he goes on PIP and will be fired if he doesn't meet his Performance Objectives during a 30, 60 or 90 day Warning, Probation and Termination cycle. If he hits his objectives in 30 days, he's good to stay. If not, but he achieves it in the next 30, he's fine. If not, but in the final 30 he does, he stays. Note that he can be fired in the first 30 days, if he fails to perform the Associate's Activities. Example: he doesn't show up for scheduled client meetings.

This is a good sample of the first page of a Performance Improvement Plan used in industry today. The second page will contain places for the employee to sign that he received the document as well as places for his manager and him to sign for weekly or monthly progress reviews. Lots of good templates on-line.

PERFORMANCE IMPROVEMENT **PLAN**

ASSOCIATE NAME: _____

MANAGER NAME: _____

DATE: _____

PERFORMANCE CONCERN (S)	OBJECTIVES TO ENHANCE PERFORMANCE	ASSOCIATE'S ACTIVITIES	MANAGER'S ACTIVITIES	COMPLETION DATE
• WHERE THERE IS A CLEAR PATTERN OF EVIDENCE IN THE ASSOCIATE'S BEHAVIOR • LIST SPECIFIC PERFORMANCE CONCERN (S) • INCLUDE OBJECTIVES AND MEASURES THAT ARE NOT BEING MET _For example:_ For the past 6 months the associate's sales numbers have been below standards for the Sales Dept. The associate needs to bring his/her Revenue and Gross Profit up to the "meets standard" level of 100-115%.	• MUST INCLUDE ACTIONS AND MEASUREMENTS TO GAUGE SUCCESS _For example:_ The associate should be achieving revenue targets in a minimum of 75% of his/her accounts as well as hitting his/her overall revenue goals monthly. • List desired competencies.	• IDENTIFY SPECIFIC ACTIVITIES/RESPONSIBILITIES FOR EACH OBJECTIVE _For example:_ Prepare and maintain an organized call out schedule and Account profile sheets for every account • Read Promo Pack to increase awareness of Current Vendor promotions to sell to his/her current territory	• IDENTIFY SPECIFIC ACTIVITIES THAT DIRECTLY SUPPORT THE RELATED ASSOCIATE'S ACTIVITIES _For example:_ Provide associate with information about his daily sales and call stats achievement. • Spend 1 hour with the associate reviewing his/her account base – help identify any potential opportunities that can be explored.	• APPROXIMATELY 30 DAYS AFTER THE ACTION PLAN IS IMPLEMENTED • IMPORTANT THAT THE ALLOTTED TIME BE REALISTIC YET INDICATIVE OF THE URGENCEY OF IMPROVED PERFORMANCE _For example:_ Present written summary of possibilities to explore within account base February 8, 2018

Download this form at: http://growthaccelerators.com/book

Pretty self-explanatory, eh? Be aware, of course, the individual on PIP will occasionally be antagonistic and determined to fight you all the way. Sometimes, they will refuse to sign the Received by Associate line on the second page. If that occurs, tell the employee that you will just send him a copy of your completed PIP document with a copy to your boss and to HR, noting his refusal to sign. If he still doesn't sign, then do what I just said.

Now, here's a technique to handle that guy who's going to fight you every step of the way. A friend of mine, Dick, who was the Region Affirmative Action Manager at my first major corporation, taught me this one. I told him that one of our Sales Reps wasn't cutting it and that he would definitely be resistant to Ed, the Branch Sales Manager's, and my efforts to turn him around via PIP. Dick smiled and said, "Okay, Jack, tell this guy to fill out the Associate's Activities section. Not you or Ed or the Sales Manager." "Why, Dick? What good will that do?" "First, Jack, if he doesn't perform those activities within the first 30 days, you can fire him easily, because he's the one who came up with the activities. And.... I guarantee you he will come up with tougher activities than you guys will." Well, Dick was one hundred per cent correct, and the non-performer was gone in three weeks. I still don't know why the guy was tougher on himself than Ed or I would have been, nor how Dick knew it would turn out that way. And, if it doesn't – if the guy submits Activities that are too easy and insufficient to achieve the desired objectives – you still have the authority to make them as tough as they should be. So, either way, you can't lose. And please understand that firing people who should be fired is an important part of effective management.

Advance Your Management Profile Step 4: Learn from the Best in Your Organization

Just keep your ear to the ground and find out who's an effective manager, preferably with the same responsibilities as your own. Then, ask about specific issues to see what she might suggest as a solution. Always try to trade something that you might know how to do well. Somebody has to start the conversation, so it might as well be you. And, of course, ask your bosses what management techniques proved most valuable to them. I guess this one's kind of obvious, yet many managers get so engrossed in executing their various tasks that they don't stop to take time to develop themselves by learning from other managers so close by.

Advance Your Management Profile Step 5: Master the Business Planning Module

This is one of the two things that has made a major difference in my management success across the years. My introduction to the need for it came when I was a young Sales Manager at my first firm, the high tech giant. The Region Sales Planning Manager would visit our SoCal branch every so often and rage on about the need for better planning. "We've got to do better planning, damn it! Better planning! Much better planning!!" No specifics – none. Finally, I went to our on-site Branch Sales Planning Manager, Dave E., and asked him what this fool from the Region was talking about. I told Dave that although I had majored in Economics at Yale, I never had any curriculum related to business planning. So, Dave said he'd majored in Business Administration at UCLA and still had a copy of a business planning module his professor had given him. I loved it and still do. It's simple, it's logical and it works

THE BUSINESS PLANNING MODULE

- **Objective: WHAT Do You Want to Achieve?**
  - — Be Specific, e.g., Achieve 12% EBITDA
  - — Analyze First to Test for Reality
  - — What Are Your Support Resources?
  - — What Does Past Performance Say?
  - — What Is Different About the Future?

- **Methodology: HOW Will You Achieve Your Objective – ActionSteps?**
  - — Example: Monetize S/W Implementation Services
  - — Who Will Do What?
  - — The Creative Element of the Planning Module
  - — Most Substantive Element, Too
  - — Prevents Objective from Being a Mere Wish

- **Expected Results: SO WHAT? What Difference Does It Make?**
  - — Broader Implications of Hitting Your Objective
  - — Help Test Value of Your Objective
  - — Example: Secure 2nd Round Financing

- **Control & Tracking: How Will You Know if You're Achieving It?**
  - — How Will You Know if the Action Steps Are Executed?
  - — How Will You Know if the Objective is Being Hit?
  - — Make Tracking Visible to Serve as a Motivator
  - — Re-plan Sooner vs. Later

Here's an example of an effective Business Plan from Rochelle who works in HR (Compliance) at a $40B+ company.

ADVANCING OUR COMPANY CULTURE

Objective

Create a positive and exciting company culture at XYZ evidenced by attracting top talent, offering holistic compensation, advancing employee productivity, and a spirit of participation, ownership, and volunteerism.

Methodology

- SoCal Flairs – spirit committee
  - o Create (already had first meeting – next is action)
  - o Branding – complete
  - o Planning – in progress
- Utilize creative communications to spread word about events
  - o Will communicate in novel ways to spread word about events (i.e. fruit w/ flags)
- Institute Associate Spotlight

- Review of benefits and benchmark against other local companies – particularly considering the concerns of millennials (i.e. student loan benefits instead of 401k)
- Meeting with Executive Leadership to discuss strategy and secure buy-in
  - Scott Morton
  - Paul Barton
  - Kendra Belot
  - Geoffrey Grout
  - Ramesh Chumber
  - Renee Olean
  - Rebecca Martin
  - Anthony Jackson
  - Thomas Harrison
- Quarterly event – 1 social and 1 volunteer based
  - Do fewer things and do them well – reign in some of the overzealous leaders
  - Require executive sponsorship for each event and ensure their willingness to attend
- Secure photo of CEO Jack in a volunteer shirt actively volunteering
- Rally support from Sr. Managers and Directors

Expected Results

- Volunteer numbers increase
- Philanthropic Committee participation increase
- Event attendance increase
- Leadership visibility and accessibility increase

- Decrease in attendance and performance concerns
- Escalate media coverage (i.e. OC's best places to work)
- ***Productivity increase***

Control and Tracking

- Track volunteer and attendance numbers
- Secure spot in OC's best places to work by 2019
- Use focus group/surveys in a longitudinal study (same associates over two year period with check in every quarter)
- Decrease in attrition at the Irvine HQ office
- Improved scores on the 2019 Breakthroughs Survey

Rochelle does a great job of taking a subjective goal and making it tangible, doesn't she? You just know this is going to work, because the Methodology makes sense, and she's going to Track it in measurable ways.

I guess I should tell you about a couple of times I used this planning module to great success, too. Back to Alaska. One of the Sales Reps told me I should get our company's largest and most expensive hardware unit up there. We were the only branch in the nation without a quota for it. I said, "Larry, who would we sell it to, the Alyeska Pipeline Corporation, one to the State down in Juneau and maybe another to National Bank? Plus, it's pretty expensive to ship it up here." Larry smiled and said I would soon learn that Alaskans had an inferiority complex about being up to date with technology versus the Lower Forty-eight and would consequently buy stuff they didn't always need. Hmm...I was intrigued by that, and so I pushed my Region bosses in SoCal to give me a quota and told them that I would make it worth their while. They said "no" and emphasized the shipping costs. So, still convinced that Larry was on to something, I called our corporate headquarters on the East Coast and got through to this older guy who was the product manager and made my pitch. He said, "That's bull that it costs too much to ship it up there. Trust me – plenty of profit built into those units." I asked him if I could quote him with my bosses and he said, "Sure, go for it, kid." Well, I did, and my bosses gave in, sending me the product with an annual quota. So, I immediately crafted a Business Plan just for this high end device and got after it. The two Sales Managers, and the local Product Sales Specialist and I reviewed the twenty-five Sales Reps' progress every Wednesday afternoon.

And it was not going well. It seemed to be turning out just as the bosses and every other purveyor of conventional wisdom had said: not enough legitimate prospects in this smallest branch of eighty-six in the U.S. We kept reviewing our faint progress with our best prospects and were just not getting the right people interested enough to come in for a live demonstration or willing to take a trial at their headquarters. Well, what about approaching the CFO? How about an Open House just for the Alyeska Corporation? Maybe get a reference letter from an oil company in the Lower 48. Boy, were we frustrated. Finally, one of the Sales Managers figured out about four weeks into it what we were doing wrong. "Hey, guys," Mike said, "this is really basic. Our Methodology is off." I asked him what he meant, and he told us we needed to just start pushing more prospects and even suspects through the pipe instead of spending so much time and effort on our most obvious prospects. If we didn't close the prospect in one month, then that's it. No more time spent pursuing it. "You can put it on a 'reserve list' if you want. Maybe we can close it later, but we're going to stop talking about it. We're going to focus on bringing new prospects into the pipe with no let-up." Well, this may sound basic to you if you're in Sales. However, if we hadn't put a plan in place to begin with and then tracked our activities and results so closely, I don't believe we would have corrected our Methodology (Action Steps) as soon as we did. Of course, I'll always be grateful to Mike for getting us back on track. There was a ton of stack ranking leverage in that high end device. We had a smallish plan of twelve. We ended up installing double that amount. And that was the major factor in our finishing first in the nation among all eighty-six branches that year. Love Mike. Love that product. Love the Business Planning Module.

After two years running Alaska, they sent me to run a three times bigger branch, L.A. South, with 330 employees. It was in bad shape, but I fault myself for taking too long to straighten it out. Finally, around October, my boss, Joe, did me a favor by handing me a Letter of Concern. That's a potential precursor to going on PIP. I say he did me a favor, because it emboldened me to do what I should have done months earlier: clean out my Senior Staff and promote better suited managers into those key positions. It's all about the quality of the people - at every level.

Then, I decided I'd better get serious about spiking the numbers, so I embarked on a Business Plan. First, I reasoned that our best opportunity would be to go all out on that same high end device that had saved the day in Alaska. That took no insight due to its stack ranking leverage. The question was just how high could we take our performance. I'm a Sales Rep by trade; however, I'd been out of the street long enough to know that I needed quality input on the Methodology Action Steps. So, I asked the top five Sales Execs to meet me individually at the bar across the street at 5:00 over the course of a week. I told them we were going to turn it around and go all in on the high end offering and that I needed their input on what Sales Activities and Results were reasonable for me to expect from each of our eighty-five Sales Execs. Well, to a man and woman, they all said the same thing: three in-house demonstrations per month and one order per month. Even in addition to their other Sales Activities and Results, they said, every Sales Exec should be able to do three high end demos per month and one high end device order. You may have heard that superior Sales Execs tend to be optimistic. It's true, and that's one of the reasons they're better than the rest of us: they aim so high. So...I examined our past performance, studied what other Branches had achieved and figured out what it would take to kick butt vs. the other Branches in terms of percentage of quota. I was stunned and thrilled to learn that I could cut the five super stars' recommendations by two-thirds and still kill it. Yup, one in-house demo per month and one order per quarter would be killer. Listening to those top Reps and doing my simple analysis let me put a Business Plan together that I believed in with all my head, heart and soul. It was then an easy task to convince Ed, our excellent Branch Sales Manager, and the several Sales Managers who reported to him.

I got up in front of the Sales Force at our January 4 Kick-off and told them all of it: how I had consulted with their top Sales Execs to make sure I was developing a reasonable plan. And how I had taken their recommendations and reduced it by two-thirds. "So, I know we can do this," I told them. "And it's going to mean superior earnings and recognition for every one of us!" Then, I smiled and said, "And I will be regarding your progress with close interest." They knew exactly what I meant by that, of course. I tracked their activities and results on a daily basis with no let up on recognition. Very public tracking = recognition = motivation.

And we *did* kick butt. The best compliment I got was from a Sales Exec friend named Mike, who handled our largest aerospace client and who had stepped down from Ed's job as Branch Sales Manager a year before because he just loved being a Sales ace. "Finnell, I don't know how you did it. When I ran Sales here, I tried everything and could never get enough prospects into the demo room. Now, you need to get a ticket, and some days it's so full you have to go back to the prospect and offer them a date two days out from your original appointment." Yes, I was fired up, and I was so convinced that our plan would work that I fired everyone else up without even trying. That's what a good Business Plan can do, and that's what expert input can do. Once you are convinced your game plan is a winner, you can spend all your time implementing with confidence and vigor. And guess what? We turned the L.A. South Branch into the Number One Branch in the U.S. See why I'm a big fan of Business Plans? They do build your confidence, and they do keep you on track.

Advance Your Management Profile Step 6: Stay Current on Management Skills and Functions

The times they are a changin' - all the time. To stay current, you can subscribe to the *Harvard Business Review* monthly. It's more "street" than you might imagine.

Shelby, one of our senior execs at my first corporation, told all of us Branch Managers to read *Business Week* page by page, even the ads, to stay up to date on business trends. I've been doing that for years now, and it's only gotten better since Bloomberg took it over a few years back. It's now *Bloomberg BusinessWeek*, and I still read it unfailingly. Bloomberg has reporters and input from all over the world as part of its economic reporting services. While most magazines and newspapers have gotten thinner, this one's gotten thicker. What's good about it is that you can be up to speed with any C-level Exec in the world regarding Domestic and International Business, Tech, Economics, Politics and Personal Finance. It only takes me about 90 minutes to read it on a weekend, and it's terribly efficient. Why is that? Because if it's a long article and you're interested, you can read the whole thing. If not, you can read the two sentence "Bottom Line" portion at the end of the article and decide if you need or want to go back and read all of it. Other recommendations I get from friends include *The Wall Street Journal* and *The Economist*. There are lots of business books out there to recommend. Makes you wonder why I bothered adding this one of mine to the field. Fat ego, I guess.

I really liked First, Break All the Rules[4] by Gallup's Buckingham and Coffman. What they did was identify the things that **employees on superior performing teams want** and expect from their managers. Their managers are providing these elements of job satisfaction. What's so great about this research is that it is statistically significant. Hey, it's Gallup. If a question didn't resonate, they threw it out and replaced it with one that did. And, again, the point here is that these high performing teams from several industries do, indeed, have superior managers; however, the survey captures what their direct reports have to say about all that. Forget all the theories

---

[4] First, Break All the Rules by Marcus Buckingham & Curtiss Coffman, Simon and Schuster

about employee satisfaction. This is what those hot shot employees themselves have to say.

Workplace Strength: Summing It Up

From "FIRST, Break All the Rules" by Buckingham & Coffman

- Do I know what is expected of me at work?
- Do I have the equipment & materials I need to do my work right?
- At work, do I have the opportunity to do what I do best every day?
- In the last 7 days, have I received recognition or praise for doing good work?
- Does my supervisor or someone at work seem to care about me as a person?
- Is there someone at work who encourages my development?
- At work do my opinions seem to count?
- Does the mission / purpose of my company make me feel my work is important?
- Are my co-workers committed to doing quality work?
- Do I have a best friend at work?
- In the last 6 months, has someone at work talked to me about my progress?
- This last year, have I had opportunities to learn and grow?

Let's go through each of these above.

1. <u>Do I know what is expected of me at work.</u> These superior performers are achievers and want to know everything about what tasks they have to complete and the best ways to do that.
2. <u>Do I have the equipment & materials I need to do my work right?</u> Ugh! This happens a lot. NOT having the right equipment, I mean. Whether it's the right CRM for a Sales Executive or the right ingredients for a talented sous chef, not providing them with the right performance tools inhibits their productivity and ticks them off, too.
3. <u>At work, do I have the opportunity to do what I do best every day?</u> Every job has unpleasant but necessary aspects. Understood. Just don't load them up with tasks that someone else could do, because these hot shots want to do what they know they're good at and that they know not everyone can do as well as they can.
4. <u>In the last 7 days, have I received recognition or praise for doing good work?</u> Okay, remember that recognition can come from any source. It can be a happy internal or external client, a teammate or a manager. As I'm typing this, I realized I should stop and thank this guy Daniel who came by and perfectly fixed my laptop this morning. I just did it. Made his boss feel good, and it will make Daniel feel good when he hears about it. And, yup, you know it made me feel good, too.
5. <u>Does my supervisor or someone at work seem to care about me as a person?</u> Even these winners like to know that they're appreciated for who they are, not just for what they are or what they can do.

6. <u>Is there someone at work who encourages my development?</u> One thing I noticed early on at my first corporation is that hot shot performers are always keen on getting even better at their job. They bear down in training sessions, because if they learn just one new thing that's useful, that makes them happy. So, working for a development oriented manager is a real plus to them.

7. <u>At work, do my opinions seem to count?</u> Tara, one of the Assistant Managers at the grocery store where I shop, is a natural leader and obviously supportive of her work associates. She's a definite "Help Me" manager. I asked her to have lunch with me and review this list and she said this one item mattered to her most when sizing up her managers, the ones to whom she reports. She said her current boss was cool, always had her back. Her two prior bosses, uh-uh. At least three times they asked her if she thought so-and-so should be promoted from boxer to checker. Her take on all three candidates was "no," and all three times she was overruled. And...all three bombed, either because they were ill-suited or just not ready yet. Tara just stopped volunteering her opinion, and she definitely felt disrespected. She knows that people can have differing opinions, but three out of three? Come on...

8. <u>Does the mission / purpose of my company make me feel my work is important?</u> Remember at the outset we talked about how effective Leaders create a vision of our work's importance? Well, I always thought so, and this kind of proves it.

9. <u>Are my co-workers committed to doing quality work?</u> This has always been a big one with me. The moment I walked into the office of my first corporate employer I

felt it. I knew these folks were winners – it was in the air, that high pitch sound, the vibe, whatever you want to call it. It's an honor to know that not just any co-worker can be on your team, and it helps you to do your best at all times. That's why it's so important for effective Managers to weed out those who are not capable of performing at a superior level.

10. <u>Do I have a best friend at work?</u> Well, I met my wife at work. And I do have lots of other close pals who are also work associates. Think about it. Wouldn't you feel weird if you *didn't* have a few close friends at work.

11. <u>In the last 6 months, has someone at work talked to me about my progress?</u> See...appraisals and regular Review & Plan sessions do matter, folks.

12. <u>This last year, have I had opportunities to learn and grow?</u> Hot shots like to keep learning and getting better at what they do. If you can help them grow, they'll love you, boss.

And there you have it, folks, the meat of what all of us want from our bosses: Does She HELP ME or Does She Hurt Me?

Advance Your Management Profile Step 7: The 5 Steps to Superior Management Performance

This is the second item that has made a major difference in my management success over the years. The Business Plan Module is the first. I'm a little embarrassed to tell you how this one came to be. I was down in the bar tossing them back with my friend Phil who was a Sales Management candidate. I was his Sales Manager and sponsor. "Hey, Finnell! Stop babbling, will you? Just write it down on the back of this cocktail napkin!"

Phil grabbed my hand and pulled out his pen. "Here, just net it out! What is management all about? What really matters? Write it down now. Just do it!" And so, I did. The next day we both looked at it, and I was stunned to see that it made sense. A lot of sense.

GROWTH
ACCELERATORS, LLC

The 5-Step Formula for Management Success

- Get the right people (hire well, fire well)
- Support them – clear out demotivating factors
- Set few objectives and do a rigorous business plan on each one
- Get all the outside help / ideas you can
- Always win (hit your numbers)

Number 1: Get the right people (hire well, fire well)

If you're a better manager than I am, but I have better people reporting to me than you do, who's going to win? I am, all day long. And I can't be that terrible or those aces wouldn't be willing to report to me.

Do everything in your power to hire, nurture and reward superior performers so they'll give their all and stay with you for as long as possible. The longer your folks stay with you, the better they get, unless they burn out. Why? Because the longer they're in place, the more they get to know your internal and external clients. They pick up valuable efficiencies that make them extremely useful to those clients.

Okay, firing. We talked about Performance Improvement Plans (PIP) earlier. I first learned the importance of firing people as a young Naval Officer, fresh out of college. I had twenty young sailors reporting to me on the ship and, thank God, a couple of senior enlisted men who knew what they were doing. There was this one young slug who always showed up late, if at all, to operations at sea like taking on fuel or taking on stores. I keep lecturing him, pleading with him. "Franklin, 'all hands on deck' means every single one of us, including you." My captain observed my fruitless efforts a couple of times. And this captain was no slouch. Engineering degree from the Naval Academy, a Masters in Physics from M.I.T. and a Ph.D. from Cal Berkeley. After witnessing one of my pleading lectures, he called me aside none too gently and said, "Mr. Finnell, we can court-martial people in this man's Navy! And it doesn't have to be for treason! Here you are, Mr. Finnell, investing all your time in this loser, and, meanwhile, you're neglecting the development of your good sailors!" Whoa...did I feel like a big dope. How naive, how arrogant of me to think I could change who this guy is. And, of course, "neglecting the development of the good sailors" stayed with me forever. That's a sin I would never let myself commit again. So, thank you, Captain Linder.

Number 2: Support them – clear out the de-motivating factors

If you've got these self-motivated winners reporting to you, then clear out the demotivating factors that get in their way. Back to Help me / Hurt me, right? Management really is quite simple when you have winners reporting to you.

Number 3: Set few objectives and do a rigorous Business Plan on each

You know I'm a major believer in Business Plans. So, do one on each of your annual objectives. The reason to narrow it down to a few is FOCUS. Three or four is just fine. I'm talking about your primary objectives, the ones you want everyone on your team or in your organization to focus on, too. If you want to throw in a few more objectives, that's no sin. Just be aware that if you throw too many out to the troops, there will soon be no focus or prioritization at all.

Number 4: Get all the outside help & ideas you can

Who cares if the idea comes out of my head, your head or my daughter's head? We just need great ideas that will work in our environment, right?

At my first major corporation, we had some brainiac MBAs in our headquarters Marketing Department. I got to know these smart folks who had such a deep understanding of competitive differentiators, for example. I would invite them out to the field to conduct a class or two with my field Sales and Technical aces. My folks loved getting these deep insights, and the brainiacs loved coming out to the real world. One headquarters guy, Paul, started to refer to himself as the Intergalactic Nerd. That was modeled after official titles like National Service Operations Manager. We established a strong bond that was beneficial to both of us. So, keep an eye out for folks like Paul who can help you with your job and also gain useful insights from you about their job.

Note that new employees will have plenty of observations and questions during their first ninety days. Some suggestions will make you fall down laughing they'll be so unrealistic. Frequently, however, the newbies will have fresh insights that you and the rest of the gang will not, because you're all part of the culture. So listen closely. You may get some useful ideas here. Of course, in three to six months, the newbies will become part of the culture, too, and be far less likely to be throwing out these observational gems.

How do I make this next point nicely? Let's just say that you can definitely pick up good ideas from non-brainiacs. You just have to be open-minded, friend. I know a Sales Manager, Kim, who had to elevate one of her Reps to a "hover" position between the Reps and her to help the Reps demonstrate and close a new and somewhat complex product offering. She just wasn't sure whom to select, as there were plenty of superior performers on her team. Her peer, Ken, wasn't nearly as successful a Sales Manager as she. A really good guy, but kind of slow, frankly. Yet, he's the guy who came up with the perfect candidate for Kim. It was Ryan, who was very bright and very technical but no charmer. He hadn't been smashing his quota, either. Making him the product specialist was perfect for two reasons: first, he'd do a great job demonstrating, because he was so bright and genuinely loved the new product...and...he could be replaced with a new Sales Rep who would be more likely to exceed quota. Wow, perfect!

If this point seems obvious – being open-minded and alert to new ways of doing things – trust me that LOTS of people are not that way. I haven't figured out why that is. Tell me, if you have. My business partner, Tom, and I would go to the huge Business Technology Association show every year and meet with other business owners to examine new product offerings. We'd always take advantage of the chance to pick up tips from our peers, to learn what was working effectively for them. One day, Tom said, "Jack, don't you think it's amazing that nobody ever asks us what we're doing well?" It was true, too. We would have gladly shared our insights with others, especially since so many of us competed in different marketplaces. Is it just ego? I honestly don't know. And that's one of the reasons I'm going on about it so much here. It IS a big deal, even if it sounds obvious. So, make it part of *your* Management practice.

Number 5: Always win (hit your numbers)

Well, business does exist to make a profit, you know. Yup, nothing evil about that. And if you operate or work for a non-profit, you will still have highly measurable goals. So, if it's a business, make sure you are cognizant of and always making progress towards achieving your Revenue and EBITDA targets. If you're in Finance, Sales or Marketing, those are natural targets for you. Some absolutely necessary business functions do not tie so closely to these primary targets. Like Mechanical Engineering which is involved in developing more effective manufacturing processes. So, my Mechanical Engineer friend, Emma, figured out that in order to advance her career prospects at her Medical Device corporation, she developed two Business Plans to attack Revenue and EBITDA head on by one, bringing a product to market six months earlier than originally targeted and two, developing a similar product in an adjacent technology. This last tenet is just a reminder to stay focused on the fact that the numbers DO matter.

So, let's talk some more about **HIRING THE RIGHT PEOPLE...**

It can be useful to look backwards in your industry or your organization to learn **What Your Superstars Have in Common.**

- **Prior Experience In Your Industry?** I found that Technical Service performance did benefit from prior hardware maintenance experience. Performance in Finance and Sales did not. May be different in your industry. Just be sure you check it out.

- **College Grads? And Which Schools?** For Technical Service jobs, a college degree didn't add anything to their effectiveness. Did prior military experience? Yes, although plenty of guys without it did just fine. For Finance and Sales, yes, it was necessary to have a college degree. Kind of obvious for Finance. You can't become a CPA without taking some Accounting and Economics classes in college. For Industrial Sales, so many of your decision makers have college degrees that you have to be able to "talk the talk" for credibility. There are exceptions here; however, a college degree for Sales is generally a wise requirement. I also found here in Southern California where I've operated for most of my career, that for Finance and Sales, Long Beach State has been a superior source for superior candidates in Finance and Sales. Why? I don't know, so I'm just assuming that since it's a Commuter School, you have to be smart enough to get in and graduate...and...you probably have to work your way through. I figure I'm getting a "character bonus" out of that graduate.

- **Age at Hiring?** At my first corporate job, I became a Sales Training Manager after about a year of selling. I was responsible for hiring and training new recruits, and I had a small Sales quota for our team of newbies, before they became full-fledged Account Execs about six months later. It was not an easy sales gig in a very competitive market, although the pay was very good. But it was too tough for kids right out of college. Prior military experience could toughen you up. And so could a route sales job for Proctor & Gamble or Del Monte or Gallo Wine. Those Sales jobs don't pay well, but they do acquaint you with the real world of business. If you find out you like Sales, you can then go on to secure an Industrial Sales job with higher salaries and commissions. Anyhow, I found that the average age of the Sales Execs I hired was 28. Nothing magic about that. It does say that 22 is too young for the Industrial Sale gig. At my first corporate job, they eventually introduced a college hire program for Sales. That means there was a quota for kids right out of school. I never understood why. Was it to lower starting salaries? Was it for early indoctrination? Beats me. I told the Sales Managers reporting to me to disregard that target completely. Business experience matters, and I want superior performers on our teams. Period.

- **What Type of Job Did They Have Previously?** This one is less statistically significant than the others, but it's pretty good. In Sales, I found that many of the Superstars had been waitresses, waiters or bartenders during college or as one of their first gigs out of school. In fact, I have hired several over the years whom I met at a restaurant while being served by them a few times. They become adept at making conversation with anyone and putting them at their ease, I guess. Actually, I think it's that you have to hustle people out of a tip in an hour or less. Of *course*, you will excel at Sales!

- **Are Employee Referrals Helpful?** Yes, with one exception, which I'll get to in a bit. Maybe it's obvious that good employees know their job and, therefore, have a pretty good idea of who would be good at it. They don't want to embarrass themselves by recommending a loser, either. And if you've got a good company or team, they'll want to do their pals a favor by introducing them to you. So take advantage of these positive tendencies and encourage your folks to give you strong referrals. Explain the reasons that it's good for them and for everyone else. Now...the only times I've seen it not work occur when the recommender is one of those unconsciously competent aces who fail to take their own superiority into account. They figure anybody can do the gig as well as they can, including their good pals. At my first large corporation, Mike recommended two guys who didn't work out, even though they were much like him – at least in this one regard: they were wackos like Mike, who redefined "party hearty." He sincerely assumed that they were just like him and would also work with his level of intensity and inspiration on the job. Nope.

- **Can leveraging diversity can help you hire better people?** Yes. Affirmative Action and diversity can smack of political correctness. AA was introduced by Richard Nixon in 1971 and required large companies who wanted to do business with the federal government to hire minorities and women consistent with region demographics. Was it quotas? No, but pretty close, and that has always irked some folks. Unquestionably, Affirmative Action had an immediate impact of opening doors for Blacks, Latinos, Asians, Pacific Islanders, Native Americans and all females.. *But guess who else made out? American industry.* How so? Simple - it doubled, tripled and quadrupled our hiring pool. You had this "pent up supply" of people who were now available to become employees in all fields of business. It was a total quality uplift. Is this idealism talking? Is this social justice talking? No, this is hard core business talking. I'm a white male, and if all I can hire are other white males or even white females, I will lose to my twin who can hire anyone, no matter their ethnic background. I saw this in action when I left a Fortune 100 company to start my first business systems company. Unless my local competitors also hailed from a Fortune 500 company that had Affirmative Action programs, they would likely just hire white guys. Were they racist? No - that's just what they were used to and comfortable with. Because I knew from experience how to tap into a broader range of candidates, I did so and rose to success based on my super-competitive Sales, Tech Service, Finance and IT teams. Affirmative Action and diversity are NOT about compromising standards - it's about raising them by broadening them.

The INTERVIEWING PROCESS for Getting the Right People

- **Two separate interview sessions** are useful to get different perspectives on the same candidate. Nothing new here. It's always best to have the hiring manager pass the candidate on to her boss after her initial interview if she is anxious to make the hire. If she's not, then why waste the boss's time? Just be sure the hiring manager is always in favor of moving forward, because she will not be accountable for the employee's performance, otherwise.

- **Use a professional interview document specific to the position.** Pretty easy to go on line to get one for IT, Finance, Engineering, Purchasing and all other positions. Here's one below specific to Sales. If you can't find one this complete and professional for a discipline you're hiring for, then contact a professional HR firm to get one. Why? Two reasons. First, you really do want to hone in on the traits, characteristics and experiences that will lead to success for you and for the potential employee. Second, the potential employee will be impressed and be more inclined to want to join forces with you if you come across as smart and professional.

ACCOUNT EXECUTIVE INTERVIEW

COMPETITIVENESS: A willing striving vs. other applicants to win the same prize, object or position.

How do you feel about activities that result in winners and losers, in some people doing well, some average and some quite poorly? Have you ever won not because you had more talent but because you competed harder? Tell me about it.

Did candidate indicate willingness and inclination to go all out and take risks to win? Being on a sports team does not indicate competitiveness or lack of it.

What is the most competitive endeavor in which you have been Involved and what were the results? How did you make a personal difference in achieving those results?

Did candidate tell about doing extra in competitive situations? Did candidate convey an insane hatred of losing?

GOAL SETTING: Able to define realistic, specific goals and objectives, to prioritize objectives.

What important target dates did you set to reach objectives in

Did the candidate show initiative in systematically setting target dates, your last job? How did you set the dates?

Exactly what were they, and what were your results?

perhaps with communication of them? Was there little involvement in or superficial compliance to hit target dates?

Goal statements are often made to meet the expectations of others. Tell me about a time when you took the initiative to set goals and objectives, even though you were not prompted or directed by others to do so?

Did the candidate show initiative and self-direction in setting a realistic goal? Was there little interest in or resistance to goal setting?

SPOKEN COMMUNICATIONS: Able to clearly present information through the spoken word, influence or persuade others through oral presentation in positive or negative circumstances, listen well.

Tell me about a specific experience of yours that illustrates your ability to influence another verbally. Feel free to use an example that involves changing an attitude, selling a product/idea or being persuasive.

Did the candidate successfully develop a persuasive approach for a one-way communication, failure to listen or a lack of willingness or specific individual? Was there a skill in presentation?

Careful listening and effective communications go hand-in-hand. Tellme about a specific time when your ability to listen helped you communicate better.

Did the candidate attend to the facts and feelings in a message and respond in a way that related to the other person's needs/style? Were there errors in listening, perhaps paying little attention to the speaker?

COMMITMENT TO TASK: Able to start and persist with specific courses of action while exhibiting high motivation and a sense of urgency, willing to commit to long hours of work and make personal sacrifice in order to reach goals.

Some individuals have a strong sense of urgency about getting short term results - others are more 'laid back' and less driven in their approach to work. Give me an example of a time when you were more 'laid back' or more 'urgent'.

Did the candidate take immediate action directed towards a specific objective so that non-task activities and interests were given low priority while productivity & efficiency were of prime importance? Was there little emphasis on effectiveness, speed or efficiency?

We both recognize that being successful takes more than luck. Hard work is necessary in order to achieve. Tell me about a time when you had to work very hard to reach your goals and be specific about what you achieved.

Did the candidate make an unusual commitment in order to reach an objective, reflecting both high effort and accomplishment? Was there a routine response to work demands rather than self-directed effort?

PERCEPTIVITY: Able to interpret verbal and non-verbal behavior, to develop accurate perception and understanding of others' feelings, needs, values and opinions; to be sensitive to and aware of personality differences and conflicts.

Tell me about a time during negotiations when your perceptiveness helped you to

Did the candidate recognize/act based on another person, perhaps referring to the match of non-verbal to verbal content? Were there snap

make sense out of another person's behavior? *judgements or stereotypes based on the other person's clothing or appearance?*

Reading people can be an important skill. At work, when has your analysis of another's motives and feelings paid off for you? *Did the candidate use behavioral observation to assess motives and/or feelings? Was there use of stereotypes or labels to make quick judgements?*

READING THE SYSTEM: Able to recognize and use information about organizational climate and key individuals to accomplish legitimate organizational goals, be aware of the importance of timing, politics and group processes in managing change.

Many times getting results requires a full understanding of the organizational climate or culture. Tell me about a time when your astuteness or street smarts in an organization helped you to get results. *Did the candidate productively use knowledge about the styles of decision makers and/or acceptable and desirable behavior in the organizational culture? Was there downplay of reading the system because of naïveté or rejection of political influence in organizations?*

Organizational change is often guided by friendships & relationships which can influence how things happen. Tell me a time when you used your interpersonal skills to build a network of contacts to reach goals. *Did the candidate take initiative in meeting people and maintaining genuine relationships to achieve productive goals? Was there aloofness or coldness, even with a person who had practical impact on the achievement of a work objective.*

94

LEADERSHIP: Able to influence the actions and opinions of others in a desired direction; to exhibit judgment in leading others to worthwhile objectives.

Individuals vary in their abilities to use power of persuasion to influence others. Give me an example of a time when you used power or persuasion to guide another person to a worthwhile objective? Be specific.

Did the candidate base her use of either power of persuasion on the requirements of the situation? Was there use of either power or persuasion to an extreme?

Communication and leadership go hand in hand. Give me an example of a time when your communication skills were powerful enough to enable you to influence the way others thought or acted, even in a very difficult situation.

Did the candidate prepare a message with a careful choice of words in order to be effective in light of situational needs? Was there some reluctance to communicate an absence of preparation or an overuse of authority?

INTERVIEW RATING SHEET

POSITION: **NAME OF CANDIDATE:**

_____   _____

DATE: **NAME OF INTERVIEWER:**

_____   _____

ANCHORS

The Performance Skills to be evaluated include:

> Very strong evidence skill not present
> Strong evidence skill not present
> Strong evidence skill is present
> Very strong evidence skill is present
> Insufficient evidence for or against skill

1) Competitiveness
2) Goal Setting
3) Spoken Communications
4) Commitment To Task
5) Perceptivity
6) Reading The System
7) Leadership

RECOMMENDATION   HIRE: _____

                              NOTE HIRE: _____

REASON FOR   _____
RECOMMENDATION

Download this form at: http://growthaccelerators.com/book

- **When is athletic success a business success indicator?** Even though I'm not a great jock, I used to think anyone who was would be superior in any business function. Just that desire to win, I guess – and the proven ability to do so. It didn't always turn out that way, and I could never figure out why. I asked Charlie, Jr., one of the superior Sales performers at my first start-up who also happened to be the former swim team captain at BYU, how come he was a winner at business, too, and some other jocks weren't. He started laughing and said, "I sure wasn't a natural at sports, Jack. I was driven to win, though. I don't know why. I just was. I was ferocious about it." Being a successful jock didn't necessarily mean anything in business, he said, and what mattered was the athlete's competitive drive as far as transferability goes. That made sense to me. Anyone supremely gifted at athletics might not have to be terribly competitive inside at all and just be blessed with natural talent. In fact, I've worked with some professional athletes who weren't particularly effective at all in business. You just never know. Look at Roger Staubach: one of the greatest quarterbacks of all time and also a major business success in real estate.

The point is to look for *competitiveness*, so I started looking for   that behavior, especially in Sales. I remember asking candidate Susan if she considered herself a competitor. She laughed and said, "Oh, yeah!" "Go on," I replied. "Well, during the summers in college, my two girlfriends and I painted houses for extra money. And I could complete one in four days, and it always took them a week - Hah!" Hired! And, yes, she turned out to be a phenomenal achiever and a great joy to everyone else who worked with her in our company.

- **See if you can find what motivates her deep down**

  It can be useful to have something, rational or not, that motivates you to achieve at high levels. In my case, it was my father's passing at a young age when I was a freshman in college. All of a sudden, I went from being upper middle class to being a scholarship student. My college was very generous in providing grants and loans, and government loans made up the rest. Still, I didn't enjoy as part of my scholarship work requirement the daily task of recording on a clip board the number of laps members of the college swim team completed in practice. Maybe it was that one of the swimmers was my cousin, while another was one of my roommates. Both good guys, neither of whom gave me any grief, but I hated it. It was very demeaning to me. Okay, spoiled brat or not, it made me resolve to move up – way up – financially. And so, my goal after college and the military was to make more money than my Wall Street analyst father did before he died at age forty-four. He's the best guy I've met, as well as being successful in business, so it was a goal that really drove me. And, yes, I made it. I did beat his annual income level. It took me to age forty-three, though, when my business partner and I sold our first business to a publicly traded firm. I wish my dad hadn't died. I'd love him to have known my wife and my daughter. However, I give him credit for motivating my butt off even after he left the scene.

My friend Martin also has a motivational story predicated on his father. And it motivates him to this day. Martin is intelligent, athletic, handsome and a business success, yet he never thinks he's doing well enough. He keeps striving and driving as if trying to overcome some element of unworthiness. I met Martin's mother before she passed, and she was a sweetheart. His parents had divorced some years previously, and the father was a lot like Martin, I'd heard, in that he was handsome, amusing and inspirational. But he frequently failed to show up for Martin's football games after promising that he would. Even when Martin was an All American in college, Dad's attendance record was spotty at best. The worst ever incident was the Homecoming game senior year. On the pathway between the locker room and the playing field was strung a clothesline with all the players' jerseys with their surnames on the back. The dads were to grab their son's jerseys, put them on and sit together in the stadium cheering the boys on. I bet you can see this one coming. Yes, they won the game and everyone was jubilant until.... on the way back, there was only one jersey hanging from the clothesline. You know whose it was. Not only had Martin been let down by Dad once again, he now had to endure the lowered eyes of all his teammates who were feeling his pain. Total humiliation. Martin has been doubling down to prove his worth every day of his life since.

I'm not saying you have to find something in everyone you hire that makes them insanely driven to achieve. You can just ask them if they do have something unique that motivates them. You just may find some things that make you even more convinced that this individual will be a highly desirable team member. My friend Latonia calls this "Finding the Hunger." I think we all understand what she means.

- **Almost forgot – why do I like foreign accents?**

This one I can't come close to proving. I always throw in ten extra points, if all else is equal, for someone with a foreign accent. Could be a Mexican accent, Irish, Farsi. It doesn't matter. I figure someone, either the guy's parents or he or both parties, had to sacrifice to make it here to the land of opportunity, and they ain't gonna' blow it. I've got lots of examples, including my friend Max, an Afghan refugee who runs the last company my business partner and I started and then sold to a publicly traded company years ago. He was a great Sales Rep, a superior Sales Manager and now, a phenomenally successful VP / General Manager. Forced by the Russians to flee his native country, his family moved to India where he completed high school. Then, they moved to D.C., and he graduated from the University of Maryland. Finally, he moved to Southern California where he's been driving himself and others to new levels of achievement ever since. And, by the way, he brought some other hot shot Afghan refugees to our company, as well. Again, this is anecdotal. I can't prove it. But if everything else is cool – track record, education, communication skills, appearance – I award those extra points. It does kind of make sense, though, don't you think?

A mid-size business systems company owner friend of mine is a Chinese-American with an accent. His theory is that in Sales, at least, the accent helps because people have to listen closely to understand what the Sales Exec is saying. I bet that's true, because I noticed that two of the best Sales Reps I ever knew didn't have accents, but they stuttered, compelling their listeners to pay very close attention to them. As far as accents go, I think it's a potential success indicator for any position including Finance, IT, Sales, Engineering, HR. it doesn't mean you go out looking for anyone with an accent. Just be aware that it could be a plus - again, if all else is positive.

CHAPTER 4

CORPORATE POLITICS – OF *COURSE*, IT EXISTS

What does Politics mean?

Some call it the power of persuasion. Maybe that's too benign. Others say it's the use of strategy or intrigue in obtaining power, control or status. Maybe that's too Machiavellian or too devilish. My friend Bob says corporate politics is simply a matter of exercising common sense and common courtesy. He's right. The Golden Rule ("Do Unto Others as You Would Have Them Do Unto You") is called Golden for a good reason: it's humane, and it works.

Someone who's known at work as a "good politician" is actually a lousy politician. What?!!? Yup, it's far better to be known as a straight shooter. The individual who's known as a good politician may be admired for his ability to charm the bosses and work his way up, but he'll never command the loyalty of those reporting to him that the straight shooter will. And in the end, all things being equal, the straight shooter will always rise to the level he fully deserves. What's wrong with that?

Navigating Corporate Politics Step 1: Ask Yourself How Your Decisions and Actions Will Affect Others

Nobody likes surprises, including you and me, so be respectful. At the first company my partner and I launched, when our primary wholesaler sent us a new Sales Representative, I told her I wanted her to always tell me bad news fast. I told JoAnne that if our main product was going to be constrained, I needed to know it ASAP. If a new hardware product was failing to achieve reliability standards during beta, I needed to know that, too. "I can always offer the clients and prospects special pricing on alternative products and couple that with a Sales Rep promotion," I said. In other words, I can always alter my plans if I know in advance even by a few days that something negative is coming down. To her credit, JoAnne always did let us know when things were not proceeding as expected so we could react quickly. That built an extremely high trust relationship, and we ordered tons of more equipment from her company as a result. Everybody won.

Navigating Corporate Politics Step 2: Recognize Good Work at Your Level and Below

I'm specifically speaking about those who do not report to you here. You always recognize the good work of those reporting to you. That's part of Management 101. This is about recognizing a support person, for instance, who may have gone above and beyond to help you out. Thank her, of course, and then tell her boss via email or over the phone what she did. The boss will love you for doing that...and...he will tell his direct report how wonderful her actions were. How does that help you? Maybe it never will. Or maybe some day you'll be trying to recruit someone who's a friend of the person you praised, and she'll tell him what a great person you are. Yup, what goes around, comes around. Doesn't always prove true, but sometimes it does. Certainly, it never hurts to compliment someone who does good work that benefits you, right? So do it consistently when deserved. Don't overdo it or offer praise when not really deserved just to win support. People can see through that, and you just get branded as a phony.

Navigating Corporate Politics Step 3: Please Your Boss, But Don't Be a Kiss-Ass

Be sure you understand all her expectations up front. Sit down and ask her what those expectations are if she fails to tell you at the outset. And always keep her informed: no surprises, right? Feel free to ask her for advice; however, you want to have your own plan thought out first. Example: "Sam, this is what I'm planning to do here. I'm a little uncertain about what I can offer as a reward or reinforcement, though. I'll share my initial thoughts, and I'd like to know what you think."

Getting general feedback: most bosses give you feedback, although some are uncomfortable doing so outside of the formal appraisal process. So, if yours doesn't incline to give you regular feedback, feel free to ask him. Makes it easier for him, and you need to know where you stand and how you can get better. This is particularly necessary when you have a new boss.

Now, of course, you don't want to be a kiss-ass with your boss or with any of your execs. It can hurt you with them and with anyone who witnesses it. It is perfectly okay, however, to give even your CEO a compliment on occasion. Not an obvious one like "great conference call today, Ms. Winthrop." But maybe you have something specific she said in passing you think would benefit the company and that should be reinforced. "Ms. Winthrop, you didn't make a big deal of it; however, I want to support what you said today about mixing up client survey formats...and...sending them out more often. I started doing that on the advice of my teammate, Charlie Grant, and I think it has upped my renewal rate. I was glad that you mentioned doing that, too." She will think about it more seriously now and, perhaps, make a bigger deal of that tactic going forward. And you're closer to the ground than she is, so why shouldn't you reinforce that comment she made? And good for you for slipping in praise for your teammate, Charlie Grant.

Speaking of conference calls, if you're working for a publicly traded company, be sure to listen to those quarterly calls so that you know what the CEO, the CFO and the security analysts are saying and thinking about your company. It will help you make more relevant contributions to your company if you know what's most important to its near-term financial and marketplace performance. Nothing kiss-ass here. You don't even have to tell anyone you're tuning in, right?

Learning from your boss's bosses can be a great opportunity, especially if they've been around longer than you. I can tell you as a former mid-size CEO and as a former senior manager at a Fortune 100 company, that most CEOs and 3rd and 4th line managers are surprised that so few junior managers seek their general advice on leadership and management techniques and practices. I do believe it's a matter of junior managers not wanting to be or appear to be kiss-asses. So, here's an honorable way to go about it. If your boss and you get along, ask her if it's okay to approach her boss for some general wisdom. "Hey, Jo, you know that I respect you and appreciate the insights you've given me to become a better manager. So, I wanted to ask you if it's okay if I try to get on Mary Winthrop's calendar to see if I can gather some management and leadership pearls of wisdom from her. On the one hand, I don't want to be a kiss-ass. Still, I don't want to be a wuss and fail to take advantage of a potential key learning opportunity, either. So, if you approve, can I approach Mary's Executive Assistant and get on her calendar? I'll be sure to tell her Assistant that it's cool with you. What do you say, Jo?"

Any reason that won't work for you? None. So, trust me that senior bosses really do pick up shrewd and useful management and leadership lessons over time. And since most of them, like me, have healthy egos, they're very pleased to be spouting off to help you grow.

Navigating Corporate Politics Step 4: Avoid Clichés and Jargon of the Moment

It comes across as fake when you're using too many "in" words or   phrases, kind of like you can't think for yourself. Some years back at the Fortune 100 company where I worked, the "in" word was "superb" because the CEO had used it to praise our financial performance during a quarterly conference call. All of a sudden, the usual kiss-asses started using the word when praising any idea or anyone. "Oh, yes, that's a 'superb' tactic," or "he's a 'superb' candidate." The rest of us just rolled our eyes. Another b.s. word I noticed at another multi-billion dollar company where I worked more recently was substituting "cascade" for "send" when requesting that an email be passed along to others. Come on, now..."cascade" this email to your direct reports?"

And avoid those too fancy "vocabo" words. Years ago, my father taught me that the objective of communication is to be understood. He said there are only two reasons to use a big and sophisticated word when a simpler one will do. First, maybe you're condensing several words into one. As an example, "reiterate" is better than the phrase, "saying it all over again." Plus, most people know what "reiterate" means. Second, maybe a "vocabo" word can refine a different level of meaning. An example might be "malicious" vs. just "bad." You may already know this: there are far more words in English than there are in Spanish, French, Italian, German, etc. That's probably why the temptation to use certain fancy-ass words exists in the first place.

Personally, the "vocabo" word I detest the most is "germane." Do you know what it means? Most people don't. It means "relevant." What else might it mean? Answer: nothing else, zip. It means relevant. So, why even use it, unless you're trying to impress somebody with your erudition? All you're convincing them of is that you're possibly a phony, eh? My father's point was that even if the woman you're conversing with knows what the word means, it's going to slow down the communication process, because she's going to wonder why you used that word. Better she be concentrating on the point you're trying to make. And if she doesn't know what it means, it's definitely impeding the communication process. Now, you can use a "vocabo" word for humor once in a while, like "penultimate." Go ahead: look it up. Bottom line, using fancy words for no reason other than to show off definitely makes you come across as less than a straight-shooter.

Navigating Corporate Politics Step 5: Emails and Other Written Material

You want to write concisely and with wit, when possible. Why? Because it makes others more likely to view your material. They start to read your emails because they know it won't take forever, and they might learn something or, at least, have a good laugh. Politically, injecting a little humor can make you come across as real vs. self-important. It also can support your objective of being understood. If they don't read your material, because it's too lengthy or too dull, you're not being understood, right?

I have an example from my corporate past when launching a printing systems product on the West Coast, home to eighteen field locations or branches. Monthly, I would send a brief communication to the eighteen branch managers, stack ranking their order and installation performance. I would compliment the achievement of the top branches and include an example of the reason(s) his or her branch was doing so well. Then, at the bottom in bold with lines all around it would be this message: "This is a 3100 copy. So clean, you can eat off it!" After a couple of times, I realized I needed to mix up my closing line, so I started asking my pals in the company for their thoughts. Randy came up with, "This is a 3100 copy. So clean, you can perform open heart surgery on it!" I remember running into one of the Branch Managers, who told me, "Oh, Finnell, you are insufferable. I gotta' admit, though, I do read your stuff, because you just might make me laugh." Mission accomplished.

I guess you can cite some example when it might be necessary; however, I think we should avoid blind copies. It just makes you look sneaky. People receiving the blind copy may wonder if you do that to them, too. By that, I mean sending an email to them and secretly copying others. It leaves a bad impression that you may not deserve. If you're in an awkward situation, the right thing to do may be to inform "another party" by walking over to his desk or by picking up the phone. Again, it's a straight-shooter thing.

Navigating Corporate Politics Step 6:
To Get Ahead, Think of Useful Projects

As discussed, it's not productive to come across as a kiss-ass fawning over your execs on your rise to the top, so think of an honorable way to get noticed. And first prove that your idea works, if possible, vs. just throwing it out there. My best example occurred early in my career when I was a tech hardware salesman in Venice, California and parts of Santa Monica. One Saturday morning, as I left my studio apartment in Venice to treat myself to a breakfast at McDonald's, I noticed that some businesses were open on Saturday, ones that might be willing to listen to my pitch....hmm. So, the next Saturday, without my usual suit and tie, I just went out cold calling as I normally did during the week. Most companies were not open for business, of course; so, I just slipped a flyer under their door and called them back on Monday over the phone or just showed up live again. It helped me get more face-to-face appointments than I would have normally. The first substantial pay-off, though, came when I sold a device to the owner of a local pharmacy on the spot. But I didn't tell my boss or anyone else, that I sold it on a Saturday. I just turned in the order. The following Saturday I concentrated on some of the tall multi-tenant business buildings in Santa Monica. The few businesses that were open provided me two major advantages: first, there was no "screen" or receptionist to prevent my seeing the boss. Second, the man or woman in the back who was in working on a Saturday was usually a highly placed executive. They seemed kind of glad to take a break and listen to my pitch. Although I can't prove it, I also think they admired my being a young dude out there busting my butt to get ahead, probably as they had done when they were starting out. Who knows? What I do know is that I got three more Saturday orders that month. That gave me six total orders for the month, which is a lot, more than the national average of two per man per month. When my boss complimented me on my production, only then did I reveal my "Saturday Selling" program. Well, he loved it and wrote me up in the company's national Sales magazine under the title, "Warm Calling." I was promoted to my first management gig three months later, and he was promoted to a senior staff position in the Western Region headquarters. The take-away here? Just implement your idea, if possible, before telling the world about it. And then adopt a non-bragging or sharing approach about it. After all, my idea certainly wasn't genius-like. But it worked, and others were able to use it, too. I got noticed and moved up. I bet you can come up with a cooler idea than mine. Go for it!

THE PENULTIMATE CORPORATE POLITICS STEP -
Step 7:
Develop a Reputation for Integrity

Well, did you laugh at "penultimate?" Just wanted to see if you were paying attention.

Developing a reputation as an honest person is the best political move you can ever make. It's the best management and leadership technique, too.

And always support people reporting to you, above you and around you when they deserve it.

Only accept credit when you deserve it. If it's not you who saved the day, say who it was. If it was you and someone else gave you the idea or the support, acknowledge her, too.

When you screw up, acknowledge it fast.

Say "thank you" when complimented. Even if it's a compliment you receive frequently and are tired to death of hearing, your complimenter doesn't know that, so don't insult him by saying, "It's no big deal, actually."

On a related topic, don't automatically return the same compliment someone gives you. My friend Julie taught me that one. We ran into each other at a business conference. I had a fresh haircut and was wearing a new suit. "Boy, you look great, Jack," she said. "Thanks. You, do, too, Julie." To which she replied, "Don't say that." She was right, one hundred per cent right. My response had been automatic and, therefore, insincere.

Okay, here's some compliment wisdom for those of you in the dating scene. Works on all genders. If a woman is beautiful, don't tell her she's beautiful, because she hears it every day. Tell her she's smart, instead. If she's quite smart, don't tell her she's smart. Tell her she's – that's right – beautiful. What if she's like my wife, beautiful and smart? I don't know. Think of something else, like she has a great sense of humor. You just want to be different, to stand out. Am I being cynical? Well, yes.

And don't lie. I mean, except for your wife or your girlfriend, your husband or your boyfriend, who's important enough to make you lie?

Navigating Corporate Politics Step 8: The Key Virtues of Honesty & Courage

Ever known someone who's always honest and brave? It ain't me, in case you were wondering. These virtues go hand-in-hand, because honesty frequently requires courage.

Now, are you responsible for your feelings, like fear or sadness? No, you are not. Are you responsible for your actions and behaviors? Yes, you are. My wife, when still my girlfriend, taught me this when I told her that her feelings shouldn't be hurt, because of this reason and that. I don't remember the issue; however, she explained that my applying reason and logic was irrelevant to feelings which just are. If you're feeling something, it can be an easy item like humor at a harmless joke that makes you laugh. Other times like fear, your emotion can be a warning sign that danger lurks. And that's physical danger which one can experience in a war zone or fear of a career risk if a certain action is taken on your end. If there's no time to think about it, you just hope you'll be as brave as those three guys from Sacramento who were vacationing in France when they jumped the armed terrorist on the train. Maybe we will and maybe we won't. Nothing I can teach you on that score. If it's like most situations, though, we do have time to weigh the risks and rewards of certain responses to the fear we're experiencing.

Start by making a list of all the reasons to go forward with a certain action and all the reasons to not do it or to delay it. And it if turns out that the right thing to do is by far the best course to take, although still risky, then find comfort in knowing ***that's why courage was invented***. Just pull it off the shelf, strap it on and go forward! You can do it. We all can. Recently, I saw again the musical, "The King and I" at the Orange County Performing Arts Center and marveled at that great line in the song, "I Whistle A Happy Tune." The line is "You May Be As Brave As You Make Believe You Are." Fear is natural. Courage is not. But courage is there to be leveraged by any one of us humans when we need it most.

In sum, my friends, corporate politics needn't be anything complex or anything that any one of us can't master. It's quite simple, really.

WHAT MAKES YOU BULLETPROOF AT WORK?

Just Two Things:

YOUR INTEGRITY

...and...

YOUR SUPERIOR PERFORMANCE

Just remember, friends, that good, caring and courageous managers and leaders are an asset to all of us at work, no matter what we do. How you manage and lead us matters greatly. Bless you for doing it in the bravest and most supportive fashion that you can.

ABOUT THE AUTHOR

Jack Finnell is a Yale grad, Vietnam Vet, semi-pro rock drummer, businessman and Leadership & Management Excellence mentor. He lives in Corona del Mar, CA with his wife, Gail. The shot above meets his criterion for a good picture: one that makes you look better than you really look. He can be reached at jack@growthaccelerators.com.

ACKNOWLEDGEMENTS

Thanks, most of all, to my long-time friend and partner Tom Barry, whose wisdom is scattered throughout this book. We spent thirteen years together at a major Fortune 100 company and then started two highly successful mid-size tech companies in Southern California, which we managed together for another twenty years. He's loyal and a highly creative thinker and possesses one of the quickest wits of all time. How else could I stay in the same room with someone for twenty years? What was in it for Tom? Beats me – my laughing at his witticisms, I guess.

Others whose helpful lessons and insights appear in this book include Larry Thompson, Steve Albano, Dave Auerbach, Bob Boyd, Jim Brown, Mike Brown, Larry Brown, Ken Brown, Bill Toney, Emma Benjaminson, Dick Bouldin, Shelby Carter, Ed Charles, Jr., Latonia Coleman, John Baker, Gary Despars, Carol Herzog, Charlie Eberling, Randy Lipson, Isham Linder, Phil Kraus, Dave Ela, JoAnn Paugh, Chris Perry, Brian MacArthur, Tom Kinsman, Mike Sidney, Guido Solares, Laura Russell, Julie Tenwolde, Craig Wiegman, Mike Woolcock, Joe Sanchez, Rochelle Breedon, Helen Vidugiris, Jimmy Si, Chris Lance, Steve Skaggs, Max Razaqui and Tara Karliner. And of course, my wife, Gail, my daughter, Annie and my father, Dad.

Made in the USA
San Bernardino, CA
08 May 2019